Jack C. Richards & Chuck Sandy

An upper-level multi-skills course

Passages

CAMBRIDGE
UNIVERSITY PRESS

Student's Book 2

CAMBRIDGE UNIVERSITY PRESS
Cambridge, New York, Melbourne, Madrid, Cape Town, Singapore, São Paulo

Cambridge University Press
32 Avenue of the Americas, New York, NY 10013–2473, USA
www.cambridge.org
Information on this title: www.cambridge.org/9780521564717

© Cambridge University Press 2000

First published 2000
15th printing 2006

Printed in Hong Kong, China, by Golden Cup Printing Company Limited

A catalog record for this book is available from the British Library

Library of Congress Cataloging in Publication Data
Richards, Jack C.
Passages : an upper-level multi-skills course : student's book 2/
Jack C. Richards & Chuck Sandy
p. cm.
ISBN 0-521-56471-9
1. English language—Textbooks for foreign speakers. 2. English language—
Problems, exercises, etc. I. Sandy, Chuck. II. Title.
PE1128.R4599   2000
428.2'4—dc21   99-058577
                                                                CIP

ISBN-13 978-0-521-56471-7 Student's Book
ISBN-10 0-521-56471-9 Student's Book

Art direction, book design, and layout services: Adventure House, NYC
Illustrators: Adventure House, Carlos Castellanos, Roger Roth, Steven Stankiewicz,
George Thompson, Daniel Vasconcellos
Photo researchers: Sylvia P Bloch, Adventure House

Passages is a two-level multi-skills course for upper-intermediate to advanced-level students of North American English. It provides an ideal follow-up for students who have completed a beginning to intermediate course, and is carefully coordinated to function as a sequel to *New Interchange,* one of the world's most successful English courses for adult and young adult learners of English.

The course covers the four skills of listening, speaking, reading, and writing, while giving systematic attention to grammar and vocabulary. *Passages* seeks to develop both fluency and accuracy in English through a topic-based syllabus. The topics are of high interest to students and provide maximum opportunities for personalization and discussion, promoting the development of both linguistic and communication skills.

Course Length

Each level of *Passages* provides material for 60 to 90 hours of class instruction. In situations where more time is available, the Teacher's Manual provides Optional Activities to extend each unit. Classes with shorter semesters can reduce the amount of time spent on Reading, Writing, Optional Activities, and the Workbook.

Course Components

The **Student's Book** contains 12 eight-page units and four review units. The exercises in each unit are grouped into two thematic lessons. There is a review unit after every three units; there's also a set of Grammar Extensions at the back of the book.

The **Teacher's Manual** contains detailed suggestions on how to teach the course, unit-by-unit notes, numerous suggestions for optional follow-up activities, complete answer keys, and transcripts of the listening activities. Answers to Workbook exercises are found at the back of the book.

The **Workbook** provides a variety of exercises that develop students' proficiency with the grammar, reading, writing, and vocabulary in the Student's Book. Each six-page unit follows the same teaching sequence as the Student's Book. The Workbook can be used for classwork or for homework.

The **Class Audio Cassettes** or **CDs** are for use in the classroom or laboratory. They contain the recordings for the listening exercises. Although the speakers primarily model North American accents, nonnative varieties of English are also used where appropriate. Exercises that are recorded are indicated with the symbol ⬤.

A package of four **Review Tests** is available to enable the teacher to evaluate students' progress and to determine if any areas of the course need further study. There is one achievement test following every three units of the Student's Book. The test booklet is accompanied by an audio cassette for the listening sections; all tests may be photocopied for class use. Test answer keys as well as complete information on administering and scoring the tests are included in this booklet.

Unit Organization

Each unit of the Student's Book is organized around a central topic or theme and is divided into two four-page lessons (Lessons A and B), which complement each other by treating the unit topic from a different perspective. For example, Unit 4 in Level Two is entitled "Superstitions and beliefs." In the first four-page lesson, students discuss common superstitions, describe superstitious beliefs from their own cultures, and complete a questionnaire that will reveal how superstitious they are themselves. The second four-page lesson, "Believe it or not," highlights folk tales, urban legends, and myths. In this lesson, students explore strange phenomena and beliefs.

The following unit structure is used throughout the course:

Lesson A
page one: Fluency activities introduce the topic of the first lesson through real-world information and oral work.
page two: Grammar exercises provide controlled practice leading to communicative activities.
page three: Fluency pages provide further listening practice and oral work.
page four: Writing exercises teach practical writing and composition skills.

Lesson B

page one: Fluency activities introduce the topic of the second lesson through real-world information and oral work.

page two: Grammar exercises provide controlled practice leading to communicative activities.

page three: Fluency pages provide further listening practice and oral work.

page four: Reading passages develop reading skills and stimulate discussion.

Approach and Methodology

Passages seeks to develop both fluency and accuracy at the upper-intermediate to advanced levels of proficiency. The course is based on the assumption that students have studied English for a number of years and have a good foundation in general language skills. They now need to extend their communicative competence by developing their ability to:

- expand the range of topics they can discuss and comprehend in English

- extend their knowledge and use of grammar

- broaden their knowledge and use of vocabulary

- speak English fluently, i.e., express a wide range of ideas without unnecessary pauses or breakdowns in communication

- speak English accurately, i.e., use an acceptable standard of pronunciation and grammar when communicating

To teach these skills, *Passages* uses a communicative methodology that centers around:

- presenting topics that extend students' oral and grammatical skills

- providing students with opportunities to carry out communicative tasks in pairs and groups that require exchange of information and negotiation of meaning

- developing students' control of grammar and conversational language through activities that present and model language patterns, and then provide opportunities to practice them in authentic communicative contexts

At the same time, the topic-driven syllabus provides a rich source of information as a source for language lessons that allow the maximum amount of student personalization and response.

Exercise Types

The following exercise types are used throughout *Passages:*

Information-based tasks

These tasks present real-world information (e.g., surveys, realia, short texts). They often begin a lesson and are designed to generate students' interest in and reaction to a topic that forms the basis of the lesson.

Oral exercises

These exercises consist of fluency-focused pair and group activities, including discussion tasks, ranking activities, class surveys, and other activities that encourage an exchange of information.

Listening exercises

These exercises appear on fluency pages (page one or page three of each lesson) and develop a variety of listening skills, such as listening for general ideas, listening for specific information, and inferencing. The listenings are based on authentic recordings of interviews and discussions with native and second-language speakers of English. They have been edited and re-recorded for clarity.

Grammar exercises

The grammar exercises focus on areas of grammar that are important at the upper-intermediate to advanced levels. These include exercises that seek to:

- illustrate how structures and grammar items that students may have previously encountered can be used in more complex ways

- expand students' grammatical resources as the basis for both speaking and writing

The grammar sections in *Passages* begin by showing how a structure is used and then take students from controlled practice to use of the structure in a communicative context.

Reading exercises

Readings are adapted from a variety of authentic sources and edited for clarity. Pre-reading and post-reading tasks allow students to fully utilize the reading passages and to develop reading skills, such as skimming, scanning, and making inferences. They also stimulate class discussion.

Writing exercises

Each unit contains one page of writing activities. In Level Two, students learn the basics of composition through various genres, such as book reports, comparison and contrast, summaries, business letters, and personal experiences.

Vocabulary exercises

Vocabulary exercises in each unit develop students' knowledge of lexical sets relating to the unit topic as well as idioms and phrasal verbs.

Grammar extensions

Grammar extensions are located at the back of the book. They expand on the grammatical structures introduced in the Student's Book.

From the Authors

It has been our goal with *Passages* to provide stimulating subject matter that will make learning English fun while at the same time giving students the tools they need to communicate in the real world. We hope that you enjoy *Passages* and look forward to hearing your comments on the course.

Jack C. Richards
Chuck Sandy

Authors' Acknowledgments

A great number of people contributed to the development of *Passages*. Particular thanks are owed to the following:

The insights and suggestions of the teachers who **reviewed** and **piloted** *Passages* in these institutes helped define the content and format of this edition: Karen Eichhorn, **ELS Denver, Regis University**, Denver, Colorado, USA; Amy Saviers, **Junshin Daigaku**, Nagasaki, Japan; Liliana Baltra, **Instituto Chileno-Norteamericano de Cultura**, Santiago, Chile; Maribel Lozano, **Universidad Anahuac**, Anahuac, Mexico; Gary D. Klowak, **CIMA**, Mexico City, Mexico; Mary Oliveira and Vera Burlamaqui Bradford, **Instituto Brasil-Estados Unidos (IBEU)**, Rio de Janeiro, Brazil; Marilda Amaral Ramalho de Castro, **Instituto Cultural Brasil-Estados Unidos (ICBEU)**, Belo Horizonte, Brazil; Gisleine Mantovani Brancher, **Instituto Cultural de Idiomas**, Caxias do Sul, Brazil; Gloria Delbim, Rosa Erlichman, Odila Jambor, **União Cultural Brasil-Estados Unidos (UCBEU)**, São Paulo, Brazil; Julia Burks, Richard Lynch, and Marjorie Manley, **AUA Language Center**, Bangkok, Thailand; Blanca Arazi, **Instituto Cultural Argentino Norteamericano (ICANA)**, Buenos Aires, Argentina; Jennifer Eick, **ITESM**, Monterrey, Mexico; Jay Melton, **Kumamoto Kenritsu Daigaku**, Kumamoto, Japan; Steven S. Cornwell, **Osaka Jogakuin Junior College**, Osaka, Japan; Julie Posinoff, **International Center for American English**, La Jolla, California, USA; Orlando Carranza R., Rubi Montejo Gamarra, Rosa Namuche, and Helen E. Kelly de Pando, **Instituto Cultural Peruano Norteamericano**, Lima, Peru; Jennifer Porter, **Language Studies International**, San Diego, California, USA; Kevan Klawitter, **Intensive English Language Center, California State University**, Bakersfield, California, USA; David Bernard Wirtz and Stephen P. Van Vlack, **Sookmyung Women's University**, Seoul, Korea; Daniel Francisco Acosta Garza and Candelaria Cantú Martínez, **Centro de Idiomas, Faculdad de Filosofía y Letras, U.A.N.L.**, Monterrey, Mexico; Demetri Liontos, **Lane Community College**, Eugene, Oregon, USA; Donevan Hooper, **Tokyo Foreign Language College**, Tokyo, Japan; Steve Jacques, **Intercultural Communications College**, Honolulu, Hawaii, USA; Linda D. Forse, **The Language Institute**, Brownsville, Texas, USA; **Senac-Serviço Nacional de Aprendizagem Comercial**, Curitiba, Brazil; Jill McLaughlin-Lucena, **Conservation International**, Washington, D.C., USA; and the many teachers around the world who responded to the *Passages* questionnaire.

The **editorial** and **production** team: Sylvia P. Bloch, David Bohlke, John Borrelli, Karen Brock, Liane Carita, Mary Carson, John Chapman, Samuela Eckstut-Didier, Deborah Goldblatt, Dru Grant, Hilary Grant, Arley Gray, Pauline Ireland, Sharon Lee, José Antonio Mendez, Kathy Niemczyk, Roberto Ochoa, Linda Olle, Michael O'Neill, Mary Presutti, Howard Siegelman, and Mary Vaughn.

And Cambridge University Press **staff** and **advisors**: Mary-Louise Baez, Carlos Barbisan, Kate Cory-Wright, Riitta da Costa, Peter Davison, Elena Dorado, Cecilia Gómez, James Hursthouse, Koen Van Landeghem, Alejandro Martínez, Nigel McQuitty, Carine Mitchell, Dan Schulte, and Ian Sutherland.

Plan of Book 2

DISCUSSION	LISTENING	WRITING	READING
• Talking about the best way to meet friends • Comparing dating rules • Discussing ways to maintain relationships	• A talk about differences between friendships among men and friendships among women • A dating service advertises what it offers	• Developing a thesis statement • Writing paragraphs supporting a thesis statement	• "Guide to Romantic Success": Tips for maintaining a good relationship
• Discussing different opinions on fashion • Comparing approaches to clothing • Discussing how first impressions are formed • Discussing how people respond to appearance	• Three people describe their approach to clothes • Three people explain how first impressions affect them	• Writing a composition about a personal belief • Giving examples to support a thesis statement	• "Judging by Appearances": First impressions in a court of law
• Discussing people who have made an impact in your country • Discussing the qualities and guiding principles of exceptional people • Discussing ways you can be a hero	• A talk about Steve Jobs, the founder of Apple Computer • Two people talk about others who have made a difference in their lives	• Writing a biography • Organizing paragraphs in chronological order • Using time words and phrases in a composition	• "A Lesson in Caring": Volunteering is an opportunity to help people
• Describing superstitions from your country or culture • Discussing different views on superstitions • Taking a survey of beliefs • Giving opinions about superstitions • Giving opinions about beliefs	• A number of people talk about superstitions • Two people tell stories	• Giving general examples • Restating the thesis in the last paragraph • Writing a composition about superstitions	• "The Sinking of the *Titanic*": Premonitions about the sinking of the *Titanic*
• Discussing the advantages of TV, the Internet, and reading • Analyzing growth in the use of media • Analyzing a TV program's popularity • Discussing the positive and negative influences of television	• Two people talk about what people learn from reading literature • TV critics discuss popular TV shows	• Writing a book report • Including essential information in a book report	• "Tuning Out the TV": A family finds out what life is like without TV
• Talking about personal tastes • Stating opinions about artists' work • Talking about styles of music • Discussing the role of music in different contexts	• A lecturer talks about Andy Warhol and his work • An expert talks about the beneficial effects of music	• Writing a classification essay • Organizing information into categories	• "We Study Music Because . . .": Why music is important to our lives

		FUNCTIONS	GRAMMAR	VOCABULARY
Unit 7 • Changing times pages 58–65				
A	Lifestyles in transition	• Describing changes in lifestyles • Analyzing how changes affect different people • Expressing agreement and disagreement about lifestyle changes • Giving advice about lifestyles and goals	• Relative pronouns in defining relative clauses • *As if, as though, as, the way,* and *like*	• Nouns related to modern trends
B	Setting goals			
Unit 8 • Buying and selling pages 66–73				
A	What's new on the market?	• Talking about products on the market • Comparing experiences • Stating reasons • Giving and asking for advice	• Placement of direct and indirect objects • Verbs in the subjunctive	• Nouns related to shopping • Nouns related to advertising
B	Consumer beware			
Unit 9 • Animals pages 74–81				
A	A wild bunch!	• Stating facts about animals • Talking about categories of animals • Expressing opinions about animals • Expressing preferences for pets • Talking about specific and undetermined time and location	• Noun clauses with *whoever* and *whatever* • *Whenever* and *wherever* contrasted with *when* and *where*	• Categories of animals
B	"Man's best friend"			
● ● ● ● ● Review of Units 7–9 pages 82–85				
Unit 10 • Language and communication pages 86–93				
A	The nature of language	• Analyzing differences between spoken and written language • Discussing what correct language is • Making suggestions for solving language problems	• Subject-verb agreement in sentences with quantifiers • Overview of passives	• Idiomatic expressions related to the use of language
B	Great communicators			
Unit 11 • Science and technology pages 94–101				
A	Good science, bad science	• Talking about scientific advances • Analyzing the effects of science and technology • Reporting on scientific developments	• Indefinite and definite articles • Present perfect and present perfect continuous tenses	• Nouns referring to scientific processes
B	Technology and you			
Unit 12 • Getting down to business pages 102–109				
A	Entrepreneurs	• Talking about hypothetical situations • Comparing and contrasting personal preferences • Expressing values and preferences in work and business	• Subject-verb inversion in conditional sentences • Adverb clauses of condition	• Nouns and adjectives referring to essential qualities in the workplace
B	The new worker			
● ● ● ● ● Review of Units 10–12 pages 110–113				
● ● ● ● ● Grammar Extensions pages 114–117				

DISCUSSION	LISTENING	WRITING	READING
• Discussing lifestyles • Giving advice to people in different scenarios • Discussing goals • Discussing strategies to achieve goals	• Two young people discuss the differences between their generation and that of their parents • Three people describe their goals	• Writing about a personal experience • Writing about past events • Providing details	• "More People Are Leaving the Rat Race for the Simple Life": Reflections on a major change of lifestyle
• Discussing successful products • Discussing compulsive shopping • Talking about the best ways to shop for different items • Discussing advertising	• Salespeople describe products they sell • Two people talk about shopping preferences	• Supporting an opinion • Writing a composition about shopping	• "Buying from Home": Tips for shopping on-line
• Talking about endangered species • Discussing ways to protect animals • Talking about the convenience or inconvenience of owning a pet • Discussing the ethics of using animals in different fields	• Listening to reports about endangered species • Reports on unusual ways in which animals help people	• Persuasive writing • Supporting a position • Arguing against the opposing position	• "Shirley and Cinnamon": Rescue dogs at work
• Talking about styles of language • Giving advice on how to tell interesting stories • Discussing problems with language • Discussing communication techniques	• Two people tell anecdotes of varying degrees of interest • An expert gives advice on how to make effective presentations	• Writing summaries • Writing a summary of a short article • Identifying essential information	• "The Long History of Slang": Slang in the English language
• Discussing the positive and negative effects of technology and science • Discussing the importance of technology in everyday life • Talking about technology that is representative of current culture • Talking about how life would be without technology	• A reporter discusses genetically modified food • A comedian talks about difficulties he has with technology in his house	• Essay of comparison and contrast • Writing about similarities and differences	• "Seafood That Never Sees the Sea": A report on fish farming
• Talking about work that can be done from home • Analyzing the qualities of the ideal job • Discussing the qualities of a successful worker	• Two people discuss unsuccessful business ventures • Three people talk about workshops they attended	• Writing business letters • Understanding the parts of a business letter	• "The Value of Difference": Individual differences in the workplace

The best of friends

1 The nature of friendship

starting point

A Read these statements about friendship. Can you explain what they mean? What other statements can you add to the list?

1. A friend is someone who accepts me as I am.

2. A friend is someone you look up to in some way and yet you can be critical of.

3. A friend is someone who walks in when the rest of the world walks out.

4. In prosperity, our friends know us; in adversity, we know our friends.

5. A friend is someone who knows you and loves you just the same.

6. A friend is someone who cheers you up when you're feeling down.

7. True friends don't drift apart even after many years of separation.

8. Good friends are hard to find, harder to leave, and impossible to forget.

> What the first statement means to me is that a real friend doesn't try to change me into something I'm not.

B Group work Consider the statements above and any you've added to the list. What are the three most essential elements of friendship?

> Complete acceptance is one of the most important elements, as far as I'm concerned. You really need to be able to . . .

Expressing opinions

As far as I'm concerned, . . .
In my opinion, . . .
From my experience, . . .

2 Friendship among men vs. friendship among women

listening

A Listen to a professor talk about the ideas of best-selling author Deborah Tannen. In her opinion, what is the main difference between friendship among men and friendship among women?

B Group work Do you agree with Tannen's ideas?

Phrasal verbs

grammar focus

A phrasal verb is a verb plus a particle, such as *up, down, off,* and *along.* Phrasal verbs follow several patterns.

Separable: Some phrasal verbs can take objects before or after the particle. Pronouns, however, always appear before the particle.

I tell jokes to **cheer up** *my friends* (**cheer** *my friends* **up**).
My jokes almost always **cheer** *them* **up**.

Inseparable: With some phrasal verbs, the object always appears after the particle.

I just **ran into** *an old friend*. I **ran into** *her* at the mall.
I always **stand by** *my friends*, and they always **stand by** *me*.

Three-word verbs: Some phrasal verbs have a particle and a preposition.

If I have an argument at work, my friend Jason always **sticks up for** me.
Because Jason is so loyal, I basically **put up with** almost anything he does.

Intransitive: Some phrasal verbs take no object.

After my friend John **moved away**, we **drifted apart**.
Although my friend Sarah and I are different, we **get along** very well.
Once we had an argument, but then we **made up**.

Some of these verbs can add a preposition, however, and take an object.

I **get along with** Sarah. I **made up with** Sarah.

Pair work Complete these questions with the phrasal verbs below. Compare your answers. Then discuss each question together.

cheer (someone) up	let (someone) down	stick up for
drift apart	make up	talk (something) over
get along	put up with	
get over (something/someone)	run into (someone)	

1. Which of your friends do you ___*get*___ ___*along*___ with the best? Why?

2. When you're feeling down, do you have a special friend who can always _____ you _____?

3. If you're in a situation where other people are criticizing you, do you have a good friend who generally _____ _____ _____ you?

4. Have you ever had a bad argument with a friend? Did it take you a long time to _____ _____ your anger? Do you ever find it impossible to _____ _____ with someone and resume your friendship?

5. Have you ever lost touch with a friend and stopped seeing each other? What are some things that cause friends to _____ _____?

6. Have you ever _____ _____ a friend that you hadn't seen in a long time? If so, did you make plans to see each other again?

7. Has a friend ever disappointed you, that is, _____ you _____ in some way? In those situations, is it a good idea to _____ your feelings _____ with the friend? Or is it better not to let your friend know how you feel?

8. Are there limits to what you must tolerate in a friendship? What are some things that you would never _____ _____ _____?

4 What should friends have in common?

discussion

A How similar do people need to be to become good friends? Do you agree with the statements in this list? Add two statements of your own.

Friends . . .	Agree	Disagree
1. should be close in age.	☐	☐
2. should have a similar social background.	☐	☐
3. should have similar ideas about religion.	☐	☐
4. should come from similar kinds of families.	☐	☐
5. should have the same educational background.	☐	☐
6. should have similar values.	☐	☐
7. should enjoy doing the same kinds of things.	☐	☐
8. should have similar personalities.	☐	☐
9. _____		
10. _____		

B **Pair work** What are the three most important things for friends to have in common? Discuss with a partner.

5 How can you make new friends?

discussion

Group work Read what these people say about meeting new friends, and discuss the questions below.

Michael

"You can meet more people and make more friends on the Internet because it puts you in touch with the whole world."

Ashley

"I hang out mostly with people from work. When you're with people all day, you really get to know what they're like and how easy they are to get along with."

Roberto

"I've made some really good friends at the gym I go to. People there are very friendly. Talking to them as you work out is a good way to get to know them."

1. Do you think these are good ways to meet potential friends? Why or why not?
2. What are some other good ways to make friends?
3. How did you meet your friends?
4. What advice would you give someone who wanted to make more friends?

A: For me, the Internet is not a good way to meet friends. I need some personal contact, not just a faceless message on the screen.
B: Oh, I don't really agree. I think you can get to know people very well just by corresponding with them. . . .

writing

The first paragraph of a composition contains a thesis statement, which presents the main idea. Each of the following paragraphs has a single focus, expressed in a topic sentence, that develops the thesis statement.

A Read the composition. Underline the thesis statement in the first paragraph. Then match each of the other paragraphs with the phrase below that best summarizes its focus.

_____ why we have a close friendship
_____ what we have in common
_____ how we are different

> ① My best friend, Ada, and I are different in many ways, but we have one important thing in common. Whenever I have the urge to go somewhere new, I can always count on Ada to go with me. Our friendship shows that people who are very different can still be good friends.
>
> ② The differences between Ada and me are significant. Ada is an artist who loves to take photographs and draw pictures of the interesting things she sees. I am a sales representative for a pharmaceutical company, and I spend most of my time talking to doctors. Ada is a very organized person, but I'm very impulsive. She's very quiet, but I'm a very talkative person who enjoys telling stories.
>
> ③ Still, Ada and I both love exploring new places. We discovered this shortly after we met several years ago. One day we were talking about vacations, and we found we had both traveled to many of the same places. Right then, we made a plan to visit a nearby historical city the following weekend.
>
> ④ Although our personalities are quite different, Ada and I have become close over the years, and we now have a very special friendship. Every time we meet, we're always full of news, and it's always a pleasure. I think the main reason for this is that we respect and enjoy each other's personality and interests.

B Write a composition about a close friend. Then exchange your composition with a partner, and answer these questions.

1. What is the thesis statement? Underline it.
2. Does each paragraph have a single focus? Write the focus for each in the margin of the paper.
3. What else would you like to know about your partner's friend? Ask at least two questions.

More than a friend

1 The first date

starting point

A Read about the places these people went on a first date. Did they make good choices? Why or why not?

Sarah: "I normally don't like going to amusement parks, but this time was different, and we had a lot of fun. We went on some terrifying rides and ended up going through a haunted house. The experiences gave us something to talk about."

Andrea: "I suggested that we go to a restaurant for dinner. Once in the restaurant, we had to wait for ages for a table. The food was bad, the service was lousy, and to top it all off, when we got back to the parking lot, it had already closed for the night."

Jason: "She said she didn't want to be taken anywhere special, so we went to a movie. It was a great choice because the movie was really scary, and she held my hand all the way through."

A: You shouldn't choose a restaurant for a first date. It forces you to sit and talk for a couple of hours, and that can be a strain.
B: Yes, but it can be very romantic, as long as you choose the right place.

B **Group work** What do you think of these suggestions for things to do on a first date? Discuss them and give other suggestions of your own.

- going dancing at a club
- having a picnic in the park
- renting a video and watching it at home
- visiting a museum

I think the best idea is having a picnic in the park. It's relaxing and inexpensive. . . .

2 Dating services

listening

A Listen to an advertisement for a dating service. What does the service offer? How do you become a member?

What the service offers	How to become a member

B **Pair work** Would you use the service? Why or why not?

grammar focus

Gerund and infinitive constructions

Notice how the following verbs are used with gerunds and infinitives.

Verbs that take either a gerund or an infinitive: *can't bear, can't stand, hate, like, love, prefer.*

I **don't like going out** on blind dates. I **prefer to know** my date.
I **like to go out** with people I have a lot in common with.

Verbs that take gerunds only: *avoid, consider, enjoy, mind.*

I **wouldn't** ever **consider using** a video dating service.

Verbs that take infinitives: *ask, decide, expect, hope, intend, need, plan, refuse, want.*

I **refused to go** to an amusement park on our first date.

Passive constructions can also be used with infinitives and gerunds.

subject + verb + { being / to be } + past participle

| I **don't mind** | **being** | **asked out** at the last minute. |
| I **like** | **to be** | **taken** to exotic restaurants. |

A Look at what these people have to say about dating. Complete the sentences with the gerund or the infinitive of the verbs in parentheses. Use the passive where necessary.

1. I can't stand ____*going*____ to bars. I certainly wouldn't want ____*to meet*____ my future partner at one! (go, meet)
2. I prefer _____ to a quiet club where I can talk with my date. (take)
3. I don't like _____ like someone special. I enjoy _____ ordinary things. (treat, do)
4. I wouldn't consider _____ on a cruise to meet someone. It's too expensive. (go)
5. On dates, I like _____ a choice of things to do. (give)
6. I intend _____ a new electronic dating service I saw on the Internet. (use)
7. I love _____ somewhere exclusive. I love _____ like I'm special. (invite, feel)
8. I enjoy _____ on a picnic or _____ things outdoors. (go, do)

B **Pair work** Discuss the sentences in Exercise A with a partner. Which do you agree with most?

C **Pair work** What do you like to do when you go out with someone special—a boyfriend or girlfriend or a spouse? What don't you like to do? Complete these statements and compare with a partner.

1. I enjoy . . .   3. I avoid . . .   5. I hate (to be) . . .
2. I don't mind (being) . . .   4. I can't stand (to be) . . .   6. I prefer . . .

A: I enjoy going dancing with my husband.
B: With my girlfriend, I enjoy going to a restaurant where we can talk.

4 Adjectives to describe incidents and events

vocabulary **A** Look at these adjectives. Which ones have a positive meaning, and which have a negative meaning? Divide them into two groups. Then add two more adjectives to each group.

absurd	embarrassing	horrifying	scary
awesome	fabulous	intriguing	stressful
awkward	hilarious	memorable	tense
disastrous	horrendous	ridiculous	thrilling

B Group work Choose five of the words to describe something that happened to you on a date, at a party, or in some other social situation. Then share your story with the group.

> This guy I went out with decided to stand up in a restaurant and sing me a romantic song. It was so embarrassing that I wanted to hide under the table.

5 The rules of the dating game

discussion **A** Pair work Look at these rules for dating. Which statements do you agree with? Why?

♡ The man should always pay for the date. Some things should never change.

♡ A woman should never approach a man first. She should always be the one who's invited.

♡ It's inadvisable to talk about your problems at the beginning of a relationship.

♡ Don't say things like "Can I see you again tomorrow?" Play it cool. Don't make it appear that you're desperate.

♡ To avoid awkward situations, let your family know where you're going and when you'll be back.

♡ It's better to go out with groups of friends in the beginning.

♡ Most blind dates tend to be disastrous, so it's best to avoid them.

♡ It's indiscreet to ask personal questions until you get to know each other.

B Group work What are the most important dating rules in your culture? Agree on five important rules, and then tell the class.

> It's best for young people to go out in groups. Two people should never go out on their own unless they're planning to get married.

reading   **A**   Pair work   Discuss these questions. Then read the article, and compare your ideas with the author's.

1. How can you maintain a romantic relationship? What are some important things to remember?
2. What problems might you face if you have been going out with the same person for a long time?

Even the best relationships sometimes run into trouble, so you have to work at maintaining the spontaneity and romance you took for granted when you first started seeing each other. Here's what the experts say about the secrets of romantic success.

Show that you like each other

Showing that you both like each other helps keep a relationship fresh. Even such simple things as complimenting your partner on his or her looks or buying small surprise gifts can help. Don't start taking each other for granted.

Keep on being polite

Treat your partner with the same attitude as you would a friend and the same way in private as you do in public. Just because you feel very comfortable with each other is no reason to relax your manners and behave like a slob when the two of you are alone.

Maintain your independence

When you first start dating, every tiny difference between the two of you (one likes football and the other tennis) seems like a potential obstacle. That's because you are looking for common ground on which to base your relationship. The problem is once you start spending more time together, you forget about the things that make you unique–the same things that attracted you to each other in the first place. Remember, it's important to develop your own interests and encourage your partner to do the same.

Commit to getting fit

Exercising reflects your efforts to remain attractive to your partner, and it encourages him or her to do the same for you. Plus, when you get in shape, you feel much better about yourself.

Take care of each other

It's the everyday things that let your partner know you care, like buying him or her a favorite magazine or the sort of snack you know he or she loves and you hate! Look for the sort of things that would make you feel appreciated. Be attentive to each other's ups and downs, too. Talk through each other's school, work, or family worries when you need to.

Resolve disagreements

Even the happiest of couples disagree over things and have squabbles. When this happens, don't think it's the end of the world. Forget that an argument has to have a winner and loser. Try to find a mutually satisfying solution. Make your point without sounding as if you are criticizing your partner. This way you can resolve issues without scoring points off each other.

B   Group work   Discuss these questions. Share your answers with the class.

1. Do you agree with all of the suggestions above? Which ones are the most useful? Do you have any additional suggestions?
2. Do you agree that even the best relationships can run into trouble?

The way we dress

 Different approaches

starting
point

A Pair work Look at these people's comments about the way they dress. Who do you think said what? Write the name of the person above each comment. Which person dresses the most like you?

| Tetsu | Teresa | Roger | Darlene |

_____ :

"I try to create a different look, so I spend a lot of time shopping in vintage clothing stores."

_____ :

"I prefer not to draw attention to myself, so I wear pretty conventional clothes."

_____ :

"I like to wear unusual color combinations. The secret is doing it with confidence."

_____ :

"I hate spending time choosing clothes. I just put on anything I can find."

B Group work Which of the expressions below describe the clothes of the people in Exercise A? Which are similar in meaning? How would you describe your own taste in clothes?

| casual | classic | eccentric | flashy | retro | trendy |
| chic | conservative | fashionable | old-fashioned | sloppy | unusual |

Describing styles

listening

  Listen to Jane, Mario, and Kumiko describe the way they dress. What are their favorite clothes?

	Favorite clothes
Jane	
Mario	
Kumiko	

3 Review of verb patterns

Study the following common verb patterns.

a. verb + infinitive
Young people **tend to wear** brighter colors than older people.

b. verb + object + infinitive
Parents often **encourage their teenaged children to spend** less on clothes.

c. verb + gerund
Designers usually **recommend wearing** complementary colors.

d. verb + object + preposition + gerund/noun
Tradition often **prevents people from dressing** unusually.

A Pair work Which patterns do these sentences follow? Write **a**, **b**, **c**, or **d**. Which statements are true for you? Explain and give examples.

_d_ 1. My parents have always discouraged me from wearing sloppy clothes.
___ 2. Girls tend to be more interested in clothes than boys.
___ 3. I enjoy "making a statement" with my clothes.
___ 4. I avoid getting dressed up if I can.
___ 5. My family would like me to spend less on clothes.
___ 6. I can't stand to waste time shopping for clothes.

B Pair work Choose an appropriate verb to complete each sentence below. Several verbs are possible. Then write a follow-up comment for each sentence, and compare with a partner.

| advise | avoid | encourage | permit | try |
| allow | discourage | forbid | tend | want |

1. Schools sometimes _____ students to wear jeans to class.

Schools sometimes forbid students to wear jeans to class. They think that students will feel too relaxed and won't work as hard.

2. Parents often _____ their daughters from wearing makeup and jewelry.
3. Schools sometimes don't _____ male students to wear earrings.
4. Young people _____ to be more concerned about clothes than older people.
5. On an airplane you should _____ wearing clothes that are too tight.
6. People sometimes _____ to shock others with their clothes.
7. Some companies _____ employees to wear casual clothes to work on Fridays.
8. Experts _____ people against wearing loud colors to job interviews.

4 Fashion survey

Complete this survey. Then add two more statements that you agree with, and discuss your answers in groups.

	Agree	Disagree
1. When it comes to clothes, women tend to be trendier than men.	☐	☐
2. Parents shouldn't tell their children what to wear.	☐	☐
3. No matter what you wear, your clothes send a message about who you are.	☐	☐
4. People should dress up more often. People dress too casually these days.	☐	☐
5. Schools should allow students to wear whatever they want.	☐	☐
6. Companies should discourage employees from wearing casual clothes.	☐	☐
7. _____		
8. _____		

discussion   **A**   Pair work   Read these two different points of view about clothing. Which one do you agree with more?

Mark

"The clothes we wear are the first image we offer. Sloppy or flashy clothing, the wrong colors, or the wrong combination can project a negative image to the outside world. I've noticed that people treat me differently depending on how I dress."

Stacy

"The best clothes are the most comfortable ones. I don't try to look unique or unusual. I just want to be myself. What's important is not the image we project at first glance. Anyone with money can buy a stunning suit or an elegant dress, so what can clothes really show?"

B   Group work   Discuss these questions.

1. Do you think it's fair for people to judge you by the way you dress?
2. Do you judge others by the way they dress?
3. Would you want to be friends with someone who had very different ideas about clothing from your own? Would you change the way you dress to please someone else?
4. How has your approach to clothing changed over the years?

discussion   Group work   Do you think students should be required to wear uniforms to school? Develop arguments for or against such a requirement. Then debate the issue with a group that supports the opposing view.

A: A concern with fashion distracts students from their studies. It also creates social barriers for those who don't have the money for the latest fashions.

B: Just the same, fashion is one of the few opportunities that students have for individual expression.

writing

In a composition about a personal belief, clearly state that belief in a thesis statement in the first paragraph. In the following paragraphs, give examples to support your thesis.

A Look at these headlines. Which headline best reflects your opinion about fashion? Why? Share your ideas with a partner.

Why look like everyone else?

Feel comfortable. That's all that matters.

Wear the very latest fashions!

Don't just get dressed. Make a statement.

B Use the headline you chose in Exercise A as the basis for a thesis statement about your personal belief about fashion. Compare your ideas with a partner.

It's important to dress in a way that makes a statement about who you are.

C Use your thesis statement to develop a composition of about 200 words that describes your approach to clothes.

Before you get dressed or go shopping for clothing, it's best to think about what kind of message your clothes send to others about who you are. No matter what you wear, your clothes make a statement of some kind, whether you realize it or not.

When people look at me and the clothes I wear, they can get an idea of the kind of person I am. I'm interested in the arts, and I'm concerned about environmental issues. Therefore, I not only wear clothes that are a bit unusual, but I also wear natural fabrics that are made locally. I don't follow trends because I don't change my basic character from year to year. . . .

D Pair work   Exchange compositions and answer these questions.

1. Does the idea in the first paragraph clearly state the writer's point of view?
2. Do the examples given in the other paragraphs support the thesis statement and clarify the writer's point of view?
3. What else do you want to know about your partner's attitude toward clothes?

How we appear to others

 Forming an impression

starting point

A Look at the results of this survey on how men and women form a first impression of someone. Check the statements that are true for you.

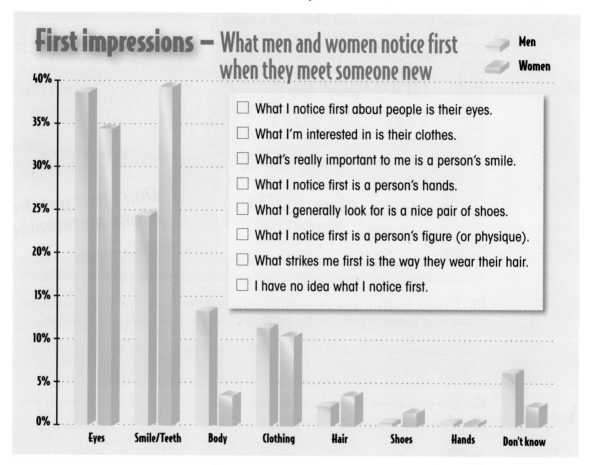

First impressions – What men and women notice first when they meet someone new

- [ ] What I notice first about people is their eyes.
- [ ] What I'm interested in is their clothes.
- [ ] What's really important to me is a person's smile.
- [ ] What I notice first is a person's hands.
- [ ] What I generally look for is a nice pair of shoes.
- [ ] What I notice first is a person's figure (or physique).
- [ ] What strikes me first is the way they wear their hair.
- [ ] I have no idea what I notice first.

Source: *Kidbits* by Jenny Tesar

B **Group work** What other cues help you form an impression of a person? How important are factors such as how people move, how they talk, and what they talk about? What are the three most important factors for the people in your group?

 First impressions

listening

Listen to Gabriela, Jung-hoon, and Alice talk about what their first impressions of people are based on, and complete the chart. Which person is the most like you?

	Something that's important to them
Gabriela	
Jung-hoon	
Alice	

3 Cleft sentences with *what*

grammar focus

Compare these sentences.

A: I notice people's eyes first.
B: **What I notice first about people** is their eyes.

A: I like to listen to people's voices.
B: **What I like to do** is listen to people's voices.

The B statements are "cleft" sentences. What do you think their purpose is?

Rewrite these sentences to add emphasis by beginning them with *what*. Then compare with a partner. Which statements are true for you? Add two more sentences of your own.

1. I notice how people dress first.

   What I notice first about people is how they dress.

2. I generally listen to their accent.
3. I look at their eyes first.
4. I ask about their hobbies and interests first.
5. I pay attention to their manners.
6. I look for their sense of humor.
7. I notice the way they look at me.
8. I notice their smile first.
9. _____
10. _____

4 No second chances

discussion

Group work Look at these opinions about making a first impression. Add two more of your own. As a group, agree on which opinions are the most valid.

"You don't get a second chance to make a first impression. What you need to do is buy an impressive suit to match the positive image you want to project."

"What most people notice first is your smile and your eyes. What you need to do is try to relax, smile, and make eye contact."

discussion

Psychologist Leslie Zebrowitz found that people are usually categorized by their faces. She gave resumes of equally qualified people to groups of business students, with photos attached. It was discovered that the students recommended baby-faced people for jobs that required warmer and more submissive people, while people with mature faces were seen as more powerful and were recommended for high-powered jobs, like lawyers. The study found that "more baby-faced people had baby-faced jobs. People seemed to be chosen for jobs, or to select themselves into jobs, to match their appearance."

Sigourney Weaver

Michael Douglas

Tom Hanks

Sally Field

Source: "Judging Faces Comes Naturally" by Jules Crittenden, *Boston Herald*

A Pair work Answer these questions.

1. Which of the people above have "baby faces"? What makes a baby face different from a "mature" face?
2. Name three well-known public figures who have "tough jobs." Are they baby-faced, or do they have mature faces?
3. In some countries, job applications sometimes require a recent photo of the candidate. Do you agree with this practice? Why or why not?

B Group work Think of at least five ways in which people are categorized or discriminated against because of their appearance. Is it always unjust to make judgments about people based on their physical appearance?

6 Adjectives to describe outward appearance

vocabulary

Which of these adjectives have a positive meaning, and which have a negative meaning? Add three more adjectives of your own. Then choose adjectives to describe these people. Compare with a partner.

arrogant	forbidding	intense	mysterious	severe	striking	trustworthy
dignified	intellectual	kind	self-satisfied	sinister	sympathetic	

Jack Nicholson

Diana Ross

Yul Brynner

Fernanda Montenegro

Barbra Streisand

Jackie Chan

To me, Diana Ross looks very striking.

She is striking, but she also looks very kind.

reading **A** Pair work   Discuss these questions with a partner. Then read the article, and compare your ideas with the author's.

1. Do you often change your appearance if you need to project a different image?
2. Do you think other people draw conclusions about your personality based on your appearance? Give two examples.
3. If you were a lawyer, how would you advise your client to appear in court? Why?

JUDGING BY
Appearances

Everyone at some point has had to worry about what to wear to a job interview, a wedding, or some other important occasion. But knowing what to wear to a court of law, whether you're the plaintiff, the defendant, or the lawyer, is just as important. It could help you win or lose a case.

Psychologists have been able to demonstrate that attractive defendants are seen as more credible, are proven innocent more often, and receive lighter jail sentences than less attractive people. But judges and juries can be biased by more than just a pretty face: The clothing defendants wear, the jewelry they display, and the way they style their hair can sometimes mean the difference between "doing time" and going free.

The influence of appearance in the courtroom is so great, in fact, that an entire industry exists to advise lawyers, plaintiffs, and defendants on their appearance. Consultants, often trained in both psychology and law, counsel their clients on how to speak, when to gesture – and last but not least, what to wear. "The jury is going to form an opinion of you based on your personality and attitude, of which dress is a very important element," says Robert Gordon, Ph.D., a psychologist based in Texas. "Whether you dress casually or formally, wear a tie or a dress, choose bright or dark colors, all make a difference in terms of how you are perceived."

"Wear to court what you would wear to church," went the old advice. Nowadays lawyers are advising their clients to wear what they would wear to a business meeting: a suit, a shirt or blouse, a subdued tie for men, and low heels for women. You don't want the clothes to make a statement. The generic-looking defendant becomes a blank screen upon which jurors can project their own feelings and fears: "They could be my neighbor," they may think, or "That could be me." Those who wear what's expected to court are demonstrating that they recognize society's laws and submit to them. That's the message the judge and jury should see.

Source: "Judging by Appearances" by Annie Murphy Paul, *Psychology Today*

B Group work   Discuss these questions. Then share your answers with the class.

1. What conclusion does the article draw about the effect of one's appearance on others?
2. Can you think of other situations in which appearance plays an important role?

Lesson A *High achievers*

1 They had an impact!

starting point Read about the people below, and discuss the questions with a partner. Have you heard of any of these people?

Harriet Tubman

(c. 1820–1913) American abolitionist. Born a slave, she became one of the most successful leaders of the Underground Railroad, an organization created to help slaves escape to the North. She personally led more than 700 slaves to freedom. Although she is not a well-known individual outside of the U.S., she is widely respected in American history.

Stephen Hawking

(1942–) British theoretical physicist. He has written about the Big Bang theory of the origin of the universe and theorized about black holes. His best-selling book, *A Brief History of Time,* is a popular account of modern cosmology. Since his early twenties, he has suffered from a disabling disease, which has not prevented him from continuing his groundbreaking research.

Pelé (Edson Arantes do Nascimento)

(1940–) Brazilian soccer player. Pelé is one of the best-known players in the history of soccer. He won his first World Cup with Brazil when he was only 17 years old. He made soccer a better-known sport throughout the world. Pelé changed the game forever, and he is considered a pioneer of modern soccer.

1. What sort of impact have these people had on other people? on history?
2. Who do you think are three of the most important international figures of the last thirty years? What did they achieve?

2 High achievers in your country

discussion **Pair work** Who are three people from your country who have made a significant impact? Make brief notes about them, and make a brief class presentation about one of them.

Name	Field	Key information about his or her life	Major achievements and impact
Akira Kurosawa	Film	Japanese Born in 1910 Died in 1998	Won Academy Award for *Rashomon* in 1951 Won Cannes International Film Festival award for *Kagemusha* in 1980

Compound adjectives

Compound adjectives are modifying phrases made up of two or more words that can be joined by a hyphen, appear as a single word, or appear as two separate words. Three common patterns for compound adjectives in English are:

a. adjective + noun + -ed	b. adverb + past participle	c. adjective, adverb, or noun + present participle
coolheaded	well-dressed	good-looking
gray-haired	widely respected	fast-talking
kindhearted		thought-provoking

A Which patterns in the grammar box do these compound adjectives follow? Write them in the appropriate list.

forward-looking	kindhearted	open-minded	well-educated
highly respected	little-known	smooth-talking	well-known
high-spirited	long-suffering	strong-willed	widely recognized

pattern a	pattern b	pattern c
		forward-looking

B **Pair work** Discuss the meaning of the compound adjectives in Exercise A. Can you think of a person to exemplify each adjective?

C Rewrite these sentences using compound adjectives. More than one answer is possible.

1. Michael Jordan is an athlete who everybody knows.

   Michael Jordan is a well-known athlete.

2. Martin Luther King Jr. had many ideas that provoked people to think.
3. Stephen Hawking is respected in many different countries for his original ideas on the origins of the universe.
4. Unfortunately, Harriet Tubman is a person few people know outside of the U.S.
5. The Mexican revolutionary Pancho Villa was a man with a strong will.
6. Mother Teresa was a missionary with a kind heart.
7. Successful entrepreneurs must always look forward into the future.

D **Pair work** Combine the words from both boxes to create compound adjectives. Use the adjectives to describe someone you know. Ask follow-up questions.

absent	blooded
cold	fashioned
cool	going
easy	headed
good	hearted
hot	looking
old	minded
open	
warm	

A: Don't you think that our teacher is a bit absent-minded at times?
B: What makes you think so?
A: Well, for example, yesterday he was wearing two different-colored socks.

Memorable quotations

discussion **A** Many exceptional people were driven by one or two guiding principles that shaped the way they lived. Look at these quotations from famous people. Can you restate these principles in your own words?

1 "I believe that anyone can conquer fear by doing the things he fears to do."
Eleanor Roosevelt (1884–1962), humanitarian

2 "Question everything."
Albert Einstein (1879–1955), nuclear physicist, born in Germany

Describing what something means

What this means to me is that . . .
My understanding of this is that . . .
I interpret this to mean that . . .

3 "Most people are as happy as they make up their minds to be."
Abraham Lincoln (1809–1865), U.S. president

4 "The really great make you feel that you, too, can become great."
Mark Twain (1835–1910), American writer

5 "We are always the same age inside."
Gertrude Stein (1874–1946), American writer

B Group work What principles do you think are important for the following kinds of people? Write a guiding principle for each person. Then share your ideas with the class.

solo navigator

struggling musician

community volunteer

entrepreneur

I guess a solo navigator's principle would be something like "Nothing truly worthwhile is easy to achieve."

  Keys to success

listening 🖸 Listen to a talk about Steve Jobs, the founder of Apple Computer, and take notes. What are three things he believed in?

  What are your guiding principles?

discussion Group work What are the most important principles you follow? Write one or two principles for each of the situations below. Then discuss them with the members of your group. Do you share any of the same principles?

▸ dealing with other people
▸ setting goals for yourself
▸ coping with problems at work or school

I try to treat everyone as my equal.

I treat people as my equal unless I feel they deserve more respect than I do.

Writing a biography

writing

Information in a biography is normally organized in chronological order. Time words and phrases help the reader follow the chronology.

A The paragraphs in this biography of Rudolf Nureyev have been scrambled. Read the composition and underline the time expressions. Then put the paragraphs in order.

____ After settling in Great Britain, Nureyev danced with Great Britain's Royal Ballet and especially with its leading ballerina, Margot Fonteyn. Nureyev is best remembered for his many beautiful dance performances with Fonteyn during this period.

____ In 1955, he was accepted as a student at the Leningrad Choreographic School and became one of its best students. When he graduated in 1958, he joined the world-famous Kirov Ballet company and became a soloist.

__1__ Rudolf Nureyev, one of the best male ballet dancers in history, was born near Irkutsk, Siberia, on <u>March 17, 1938</u>. As a child he loved dancing and music. He began dancing with an amateur folk-dance group when he was eight years old.

____ From 1983 to 1989, Nureyev worked as the director of the Paris Opera Ballet Theater. During this period, Nureyev staged many wonderful ballets. He died in 1993.

____ While visiting Paris with the Kirov Ballet in 1961, Nureyev decided to leave his career in Russia behind and pursue a new life in Western Europe. He published his autobiography the following year and went on to dance with many famous ballet companies in Great Britain, other European countries, the United States, and Australia.

B Put this information about athlete Michael Jordan in chronological order. Then use the information to write a biography of several paragraphs. Include additional information if you can, and comment on Michael Jordan's achievements.

____ enrolled at the University of North Carolina in 1980

____ returned to the National Basketball Association (NBA) in March 1995

__1__ was born Michael Jeffrey Jordan in Brooklyn, New York, on February 17, 1963

____ retired from basketball in 1999

____ quickly became the NBA's Most Valuable Player (MVP) and would win the title six times

____ in 1984, played on the U.S. Olympic basketball team that won the gold medal

____ also in 1984, joined the NBA as a player for the Chicago Bulls

____ won the National Basketball Championship as a college freshman

____ retired before the 1993–94 season to pursue a baseball career

____ decided that he would never excel at professional baseball

C Pair work Exchange papers with a partner, and answer these questions.

1. Did your partner organize the information chronologically?
2. What are the strengths of your partner's composition? Do you have any suggestions for improvement?

Role models

starting point **A** Read the article and discuss the questions below.

Mike Tidwell, a Peace Corps volunteer in the Democratic Republic of Congo, was very much influenced by a village chief named Ilunga, who had asked him for advice on how to raise fish. Mike sold Ilunga a shovel, and Ilunga then spent two months digging a pond to hold the fish.

"There is no easy way to dig a fish pond with a shovel. You just have to do it. For me it was painful visiting Ilunga each week. I winced each time his foot pushed the shovel into the ground. I calculated that to finish the pond, he would have to move a total of 4,000 cubic feet of dirt. One week I couldn't stand it any longer. 'Give me the shovel,' I told him. But after just two hours of digging, I was incapable of doing any more. Day after day, four or five hours each day, Ilunga kept going. Finally, there it was: Ilunga's pond – huge, about 45 by 60 feet, and completely finished. Ilunga had done it. And when we finally stocked the pond, I knew that no man would ever command more respect from me than one who, to better feed his children, moves 4,000 cubic feet of dirt with a shovel. I had a hero."

–*Mike Tidwell*

1. Why do you think the writer admires Ilunga so much?
2. In your opinion, what kind of person is Ilunga?
3. Have you ever met someone who had a strong influence on you? How did they influence you?

B Complete these statements with information about people you know. Share your information with the class.

1. The most generous person I know is . . .
2. The most influential person in my life was . . .
3. The most inspiring person I've ever met is . . .
4. Of all my family, . . . is the most . . .

People who made a difference

listening Listen to Luisa and Jun describe how other people made a difference in their lives, and complete the chart.

	Who influenced them	In what way
Luisa		
Jun		

3

grammar focus

Superlative adjectives

Superlative adjectives usually appear before the noun they modify.

The funniest person I know is my friend Bob.
The most caring individual in our school is the custodian.

They can also occur without the noun they modify.

Of all the people in my family, my aunt Ruth is **the kindest**.
Of all my professors, Dr. Lopez is **the most inspiring**.

Superlatives are often followed by relative clauses in the present perfect.

My cousin Anita is **the most generous** person **I've ever met**.
The closest friend **I've ever had** is someone I met in elementary school.

A Complete these sentences with your own information, and add more details. Then compare with a partner.

1. One of the most inspiring people I've ever known is . . .

   One of the most inspiring people I've ever known is my math teacher.
   She encourages students to think rather than just memorize formulas and rules.

2. The most successful individual I know is . . .
3. Of all the people I know, . . . is the least self-centered.
4. The youngest person who I consider to be a hero is . . .
5. The most moving speaker I have ever heard is . . .
6. The most important role model I've ever had is . . .
7. Of all the friends I've ever had, . . . is the most understanding.
8. One of the bravest things I've ever done is . . .

B Use the superlative form of these adjectives to describe people you admire. Write at least five sentences.

brave	honest	interesting	smart
generous	inspiring	kind	witty

My next-door neighbor is the bravest person I've ever met.

C Group work Discuss the sentences you wrote in Exercises A and B. Ask each other follow-up questions.

A: My next-door neighbor is the bravest person I've ever met.
B: What did your neighbor do, exactly?
A: She's a firefighter, and once she saved a child from a burning building. . . .

4 Everyday heroism

discussion **A Pair work** Read what this person says about heroic behavior. What is this person's definition of a hero? Do you agree with the definition?

> To me, a hero is not only someone who saves a person from a burning building. It could be a parent who, after an exhausting day, helps a child with a difficult homework assignment. It could be a person on the street who picks up and returns something you didn't realize you'd dropped, someone who stops by to check on you when you're ill, someone who calms you down when you're angry, someone who takes time out of a busy schedule to help you with a problem. A hero is not just a person who has the courage to take a risk; he or she is also a person who has the courage to always be kind to people in every situation.

B Group work Discuss these questions.

1. Can you add three more examples of everyday heroism?
2. Has someone been a hero to you recently? Describe what happened.
3. Have you been a hero to someone lately? What did you do?

5 Phrasal verbs

vocabulary Complete the sentences with these phrasal verbs. If you are not sure how they function grammatically, look back at the Grammar Focus on page 3. Can you define the meaning of the verbs in your own words?

calm (someone) down   follow through on   sit down
care for (someone)   get along with   stop/drop by
check on (someone/something) give (something) away
come through for   pick (someone/something) up

1. Sometimes my colleagues at work get upset about things, but my supervisor always _____sits_____ _____down_____ with us to discuss the problem and manages to _____calm_____ everyone _____down_____.
2. My mother is very easygoing, so she _____ _____ _____ just about everyone.
3. I have a very generous uncle who is always _____ his money _____ to charities that he believes in. He also volunteers at a hospital where he helps _____ _____ sick children.
4. When I had the flu recently, a friend of mine _____ _____ several times to _____ _____ me and see if I was OK. He went out and _____ _____ food and medicine for me. I admire people who really _____ _____ _____ their friends when they need help.
5. Some people offer to do things for you and then never _____ _____ _____ their promises.

6 You can be a hero

discussion Discuss these situations. What would you do to make a difference?

Your next-door neighbor fell and broke her leg. She lives by herself.	The condition of your neighborhood park has deteriorated, and fewer and fewer people are using it.	Children in a nearby low-income neighborhood seem to have few opportunities for academic success.	A friend of yours has lost his or her job and can't seem to find another one.

> *I would offer to pick up groceries for my neighbor and help her out with the housework.*

reading **A** **Pair work** Discuss these questions. Then read the article, and compare your ideas with the author's.

1. Why do you think some people volunteer to help others?
2. Do you think people who volunteer to help others are heroes? Why or why not?
3. What are some ways that volunteering to help someone else might help the volunteer?

A Lesson in Caring

I didn't even notice him. It was a chilly November evening in New York City, and my daughter and I were walking up Broadway. I was thinking, "Milk, dry cleaners, home." Was I supposed to notice a guy sitting inside a cardboard box next to a newsstand? No, but Nora did. She wasn't even four, but she pulled at my coat sleeve and said, "That man's cold, Daddy. Can we take him home?"

I don't remember my reply – probably something like, "That wouldn't really be helping him." Maybe I made her feel better by giving her an apple. I don't know. But I do remember a sudden heavy feeling inside me. I had always been delighted at how much my daughter noticed in her world, whether it was birds in flight or children playing. But now she was noticing suffering and poverty.

A few days later, I saw an article in the newspaper about volunteers who delivered meals to elderly people. The volunteers went to a nearby school on a Sunday morning, picked up a food package, and delivered it to an elderly person. It was quick and easy. I signed us up. Nora was excited about it. She could understand the importance of food, so she could easily see how valuable our job was. When Sunday came, she was ready, but I had to push myself to leave the house. On the way to the school, I fought an urge to turn back. The Sunday paper and my coffee were waiting at home. Why do this? Still, we picked up the package and phoned the elderly person we'd been assigned. She invited us right over.

The building was depressing. I remember thinking, "No one knows we're doing this. We can still go home." Then the door opened. Facing us was a silver-haired woman in an old dress. She took the package and asked if we would like to come in. Nora ran inside. I reluctantly followed. Once inside, I saw the apartment belonged to someone poor. Our hostess showed us some photos of her family and some travel souvenirs. Nora played and laughed. I accepted a second cup of tea. When it came time to say good-bye, we three stood in the doorway and hugged. I walked home in tears.

Professionals call such a visit a "volunteer opportunity." They are opportunities, I've come to see. Where else but as volunteers do you have the opportunity to do something enjoyable that's good for others as well as for yourself? Indeed, the poverty my daughter and I helped lessen that Sunday afternoon was not the old woman's alone – it was in our lives, too. Nora and I regularly serve meals to needy people and collect clothes for the homeless. Yet, as I've watched her grow over these past four years, I still wonder – which of us has benefited more?

Source: "A Lesson in Caring" by Teddy Gross, *Sesame Street Parents*

B **Group work** Discuss these questions. Then share your answers with the class.

1. In what way do you think the author and his daughter benefited from the visits?
2. What do you think motivated the author to begin doing volunteer work?
3. Would you consider the author a hero? Why or why not?

1 Phrasal verbs

A Complete these phrasal verbs with the particles *up, down, through,* or *away.* In several cases, there is more than one possibility.

calm ___down___   follow _____ on   let _____   put _____ with
cheer _____   give _____   pick _____   stick _____ for

B Complete these sentences using one of the phrasal verbs above.

1. Whenever I feel nervous, I find that listening to music ___calms___ me ___down___, and when I'm depressed, it _____ me _____.
2. I can _____ _____ _____ a lot of things, but I can't tolerate dishonesty from a friend.
3. When you promise to do something, it's important to _____ _____ _____ your commitment.
4. When you're being unfairly attacked, good friends should take your side and _____ _____ _____ you if necessary.
5. When my best friend gets sick, I always try to help her out, so I do things like _____ _____ groceries at the store. When I need help, I can count on her, too. She never _____ me _____.
6. I don't have enough room in my closets, so I'm planning to _____ some of my clothes _____ to my friends.

2 Gerund and infinitive constructions

A Which of these verbs are followed by gerunds only? Which are followed by infinitives only? Which are followed by either gerunds or infinitives?

ask	can't stand	enjoy	hope	love	plan	want
avoid	consider	expect	intend	mind	prefer	would like
can't bear	decide	hate	like	need	refuse	

gerunds	infinitives	gerunds or infinitives
	ask	

B Mark these sentences active (A) or passive (P). If necessary, rewrite them so that they're true for you. Give reasons.

__P__ 1. I like being taken out to dinner.

   I can't stand being taken out to dinner. I prefer paying for myself.

_____ 2. I hate to go on a date with another couple.
_____ 3. I intend to remain single until I'm in my thirties.
_____ 4. I refuse to go to the movies on a first date.
_____ 5. I can't bear to be invited to a dinner party.
_____ 6. I consider going to an amusement park an exciting first date.
_____ 7. I love being complimented on my appearance.

3 Review of verb patterns

Which of the verb patterns below do these sentences follow? Write the letter next to the sentence. Then complete the chart with two sentences of your own for each pattern.

- _a_ 1. I tend to dress in dark colors.
- ____ 2. I try to follow the latest fashions.
- ____ 3. I never permit myself to buy clothes I don't really need.
- ____ 4. I enjoy wearing comfortable clothes.
- ____ 5. My family prevents me from following the latest fashions.
- ____ 6. I avoid dressing in a flashy way.
- ____ 7. I usually encourage my friends to dress sensibly.
- ____ 8. I discourage my friends from copying my style.

a. verb + infinitive	
b. verb + object + infinitive	
c. verb + gerund	
d. verb + object + preposition + gerund/noun	

4 Cleft sentences with **what**

A Rewrite these sentences using cleft sentences with *what*.

1. I pay attention to the way people dress.

   What I pay attention to is the way people dress.

2. I notice the way someone walks.
3. I expect that the people I date will give me compliments about my appearance.
4. I am attracted to a person's intelligence.
5. I generally look at the way a person stands.
6. I am not interested in a person's educational background.
7. I don't pay attention to a person's physical appearance.

B Pair work What's your advice about these situations? Complete the sentences and then discuss with a partner.

1. When you first meet someone, what's most important . . .

   When you meet someone, what's most important is to look friendly and relaxed.

2. If I go out to a restaurant with someone, what I pay attention to . . .
3. Whenever my best friend is feeling down, what I like to do . . .
4. When I meet someone for the first time, what I try to wear . . .

5

Compound adjectives

A Put these compound adjectives in the correct column below. Then add two more compound adjectives of your own to each column.

absent-minded	fast-thinking	warmhearted
awe-inspiring	old-fashioned	well-educated
easygoing	single-minded	widely acclaimed

adjective + noun + -ed	adverb + past participle	adjective, adverb, or noun + present participle
absent-minded		

B Pair work Think of six people who have had a major impact on life in your country. Write sentences about them using the compound adjectives below or others of your own.

coldhearted	strong-willed
coolheaded	universally recognized
forward-looking	warmhearted
single-minded	well-respected

6

Superlative adjectives

A Complete these sentences with your own information. Add reasons for your opinions, and compare with a partner.

1. The most understanding person in my family is . . .
2. Of all the people I know, the most successful is . . .
3. The most rewarding relationship I've ever had is . . .
4. One of the most inspiring things I've ever seen is . . .
5. The most influential person in my neighborhood is . . .
6. The bravest person I've ever met is . . .

B Pair work Who are some people you admire? Use the superlative form of these adjectives to write sentences about them. Give reasons.

| caring | generous | honest | supportive |
| fascinating | heroic | kind | understanding |

My sister Suzanne is the most caring person I've ever met. She's always . . .

Personal examples

Pair work Give personal examples for these items. Then discuss with a partner.

something you would enjoy or couldn't stand doing on a first date	something you encourage your friends to do or discourage them from doing	something you mind/don't mind being asked to do by a friend	something you would agree to/refuse to put up with in a love relationship

8 Attitudes about fashion

Group work Choose the four statements about clothing you agree with most, and discuss in your group. Then share your answers with the class.

▸ What you wear is who you are.

▸ People often discriminate against others because of the way they dress.

▸ It's more important to dress comfortably than fashionably.

▸ People tend to think less about fashion as they get older.

▸ When you buy clothes, it's more important to think about quality than price or style.

▸ Young people should avoid following fashion trends.

▸ Parents shouldn't permit their children to wear shocking clothes.

▸ People who dress unfashionably have a more difficult time making friends.

9 Personal principles

Pair work Read what these people say about their personal guiding principles. Who is most similar to you, and who is least similar?

Lucas

"What guides me is the idea that you never know what's going to happen, and you need to be ready to face up to problems and take advantage of opportunities. Life is full of surprises, and I always look forward to finding out what they are."

Sandra

"I feel it's important to hold on to your dreams, no matter how difficult things get. I don't want to get older and find that I have regrets about my life because I gave up too easily."

Allen

"My guiding principle is 'Be laid back and take life just as it comes.' No one ever gets anywhere by worrying too much about the future. I try to just take one day at a time."

Lesson A *Superstitions*

1 The things people believe!

starting point

Read the list of common superstitions and beliefs. Which ones do some people in your country believe in? Do you know any other superstitions?

1. It is said that amber beads worn around the neck can protect you against illness.
2. If you make a wish and then blow out all the candles on your birthday cake on your first try, your wish will come true.
3. Some people claim that you should never take a broom with you when you move to a new house. Throw it out and buy a new one.
4. Many people believe that breaking a mirror will bring you seven years of bad luck.
5. Farmers in some countries believe that a cricket in the house brings good luck.
6. In the U.S. it is sometimes said that if your right ear itches, someone is saying good things about you.
7. Many people admit that they would never start a trip on a Friday.
8. If a black cat walks toward you, it will bring you good luck.

> I think many people believe that breaking a mirror will bring bad luck.

> Really? I've never heard that one.

2 Common superstitions

listening

 Listen to people talking about superstitions, and complete the chart. What is an explanation for each superstition?

Superstition	Explanation

3 Reporting clauses

grammar focus

To report what someone says or thinks, you can use these verbs to introduce a *that* clause. The use of *that* is optional.

admit   argue   assume   claim   explain   report
agree   assert   believe   doubt   feel   say

In many countries, people **believe (that)** breaking a mirror brings you seven years of bad luck. Not many people like to **admit (that)** they are superstitious.

A Pair work Read the following statements about superstitions and beliefs, and tell a partner what you think about them. Use these verbs in your sentences.

agree   assume   believe   doubt   feel

1. Carrying a good luck charm will protect you from harm.
2. Only uneducated people still believe in superstitions.
3. Crystals have mysterious healing powers.
4. Almost everyone is superstitious about a few things.
5. There is some truth behind every superstition.
6. Superstitions are dangerous because they prevent people from thinking scientifically.
7. Superstitions are an important part of our cultural heritage.
8. To avoid any problems, you should follow traditional rituals and customs when planning your wedding.

> *I doubt very much that carrying a good luck charm will protect you from harm.*

B Pair work Write six statements of your own using the verbs from the grammar box and a *that* clause. Compare your answers with a partner.

Many people believe that superstitions are dangerous, but I believe that they add interest and fun to life.

4 Everyday superstitions

discussion

A Pair work Do you know any superstitions connected with these things?

animals   food
clothing   household objects
colors   money
days, dates, or months numbers

B Group work Join another pair and compare your answers. Ask follow-up questions.

A: My grandparents believe that it's bad luck to get married on a Tuesday.
B: Do other people in your family believe that?
A: I think my mother does.
C: Really? What do they say is a good day to get married?

discussion   **A** **Pair work** Take turns interviewing each other, and complete the questionnaire. Then calculate your scores.

	Yes	No
1. Do you have a piece of clothing that brings you good luck?	☐	☐
2. Are there any particular days that you consider unlucky?	☐	☐
3. Do you have any lucky numbers?	☐	☐
4. Do you think some colors bring good luck?	☐	☐
5. Do you avoid walking under a ladder because it might bring you bad luck?	☐	☐
6. Are there any animals you consider unlucky?	☐	☐
7. Do you believe that certain actions before a wedding bring good or bad luck?	☐	☐
8. Do you carry any good luck charms?	☐	☐
9. Do you keep any good luck charms in your house?	☐	☐
10. Do you avoid having specific items in your house because they might bring bad luck?	☐	☐

Score

8–10 Wow! You're really superstitious!   2–4 You're not very superstitious, but . . .

5–7   You're fairly superstitious, aren't you?   0–1 Life is not a matter of luck to you!

B **Group work** Compare your scores. Then explain some of the things you're superstitious about. Is there anything else that you think brings good or bad luck?

> Have you ever heard the expression "knock on wood"? If you knock on something made of wood, you'll continue to have good luck with whatever you're talking about.

discussion   **Group work** Read these statements. Who do you agree with most, and who do you agree with least? Why?

Angela

"People who have superstitions seem to feel that the world is ruled by chance. This is, as we all know, completely false."

Andrew

"Before you claim that superstitions are silly, you should study their origins. Many superstitions regarding health, for example, have some truth to them."

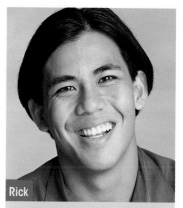

Rick

"Many people say that they are not superstitious, but I don't believe there's anyone alive who doesn't have at least a couple of superstitious beliefs."

> I agree most with Rick. I believe that everyone has at least a few superstitions. . . .

writing

The first paragraph of a composition provides the thesis statement and sometimes gives general examples. The last paragraph restates the thesis statement.

A Read this composition. Find the thesis statement and a supporting example in the first paragraph. Then look at the last paragraph. Which sentence restates the thesis statement?

Some people think that certain objects bring them good luck; others avoid certain things or situations that they believe might bring them bad luck. Even people who claim not to believe in superstitions sometimes use phrases such as "Keep your fingers crossed" when they speak. Superstitions concerning both good and bad luck are part of everyone's life in the United States. Even if you don't believe in them, they are difficult to ignore.

It's easy to find superstitions relating to good luck. For example, my friend Irene carries a rabbit's foot in her pocket to bring her good luck. Another friend who plays baseball panics whenever his mother washes his "lucky" baseball socks. My mother believes that nine is her lucky number, and even my levelheaded father has hung a horseshoe over the entrance of our home to bring us good luck and good fortune.

Superstitions concerning bad luck are just as common. My mother believes that certain days are bad for events like marriages and ceremonies, while my uncle always knocks on wood to keep bad luck from happening to him. Then there's my friend who goes out of his way to avoid black cats. My sister never puts her bag on the floor because she thinks doing so will bring her bad luck.

Personally, I am not very superstitious. I don't have any lucky socks, and I don't have any lucky or unlucky numbers. Still, I find myself avoiding black cats and crossing my fingers for my friends. Superstitions are just a part of life, whether or not you believe in them.

B Write a composition about superstitions and good and bad luck in your culture. Do your first and last paragraphs follow the guidelines stated in the box?

C **Pair work** Exchange your composition with a partner, and answer these questions.

1. Does the first paragraph contain a thesis statement and give general examples?
2. How well do the examples in the middle paragraphs support the thesis? Are there enough examples?
3. Does the last paragraph restate the thesis?

Believe it or not

1 Fact or fiction?

starting point

A Read these stories from tabloid newspapers, and rate them from 1 to 4 (1 = probably true, 2 = plausible, 3 = unlikely, 4 = unbelievable).

A woman in Spain says she has been receiving messages from her husband, who died 20 years ago. It is reported that the woman receives messages once a week in the form of voices that speak to her in dreams. ☐

Villagers in Cambodia have discovered a cow that they believe is sacred and can cure illnesses. It is claimed that the cow has cured over 100 people with serious illnesses by licking the affected area. ☐

A family living in an old house in England has made a video of a ghost that appears in the house at night. It is believed that the ghost is that of a man who lived in the house 200 years ago and disappeared one day without a trace. ☐

A couple in the United States reported that they were driving along a country road at 10:00 P.M. when they were blinded by a very bright light in the sky. The next thing they remember is that they woke up at 6:00 A.M. – 300 miles away. They believe they were abducted by aliens. ☐

B Group work Discuss these questions.

1. How would you explain the events in each story?
2. Why do you think tabloid newspapers containing stories like these are so popular?
3. Have you heard of any unusual stories like the ones above? Share them with the group.

2 Talking about strange phenomena

vocabulary Pair work Complete these sentences with words from the list below. Then compare your answers with a partner.

alien	ESP (extrasensory perception)	psychic	UFO (unidentified flying object)
astrology	ghost	telepathy	

1. A ___psychic___ is someone who has the power to predict the future or to see things that are not present. They sometimes help solve crimes.
2. _____ is the ability to "read a person's mind" simply by using mental powers.
3. An _____ is a creature from outer space – an inhabitant of another planet or galaxy.
4. A _____ is a spirit of someone who has died.
5. A "flying saucer" is an example of a _____, a strange object people sometimes see in the sky.
6. _____ is the ability to gain information using special mental powers instead of the five senses.
7. _____ studies the influence of stars and planets on human nature. Astrological signs affect people's character and personality.

Reporting clauses in the passive

To report a claim or opinion, you can use a passive form of a reporting verb and *it*. Notice that the agent is often omitted and understood to be "some" or "many people."

It is reported that a woman from Spain receives messages once a week from her dead husband.
It is believed that a cow in Cambodia has cured over 100 people.
It has been claimed by many people that the cow had extraordinary powers.
It was once believed that the earth was flat.

A Rewrite these statements with a passive form of the verb and *it*.

1. People assume that some people report alien abductions to get publicity.

It is assumed that some people report alien abductions to get publicity.

2. People estimate that 50 percent of the population believes in ghosts.
3. Many people have said that UFO sightings are increasing.
4. Many people believe that some people have experienced telepathy.
5. Many claim that some people can communicate with plants.
6. Some people used to say that Mars was inhabited by aliens.
7. People say that many celebrities consult astrologers.

B Pair work Complete these statements about beliefs using your own information. Add two more statements of your own, and compare your statements with a partner.

▶ People don't believe this anymore, but it used to be said that . . .
▶ Recently, it has been reported in the news that . . .
▶ Several years ago, it was rumored that a celebrity . . .
▶ _____
▶ _____

Survey of beliefs

A Pair work Complete the chart. Then discuss your answers with a partner.

	Agree	Disagree	Not sure
1. Psychics have been able to locate crime victims using extrasensory perception.	☐	☐	☐
2. UFOs are real and many people have seen them.	☐	☐	☐
3. Governments don't want people to know the truth about UFOs.	☐	☐	☐
4. People's lives are affected by their astrological signs.	☐	☐	☐
5. Some people can use telepathy to "read other people's minds."	☐	☐	☐

B Group work Compare your answers. Which statements do most of the people in your group agree with?

I don't believe that psychics have any special powers.

I don't agree. It was reported last year that a psychic helped the police find the body of a murder victim.

discussion **A** Read these stories and match them with the definitions on the right. Check your answers on page 118.

1 The world rests on the back of giant catfish. When the catfish quarrel or get hungry, they move around. The result is an earthquake. Japan

a. legend A story handed down for generations about a larger-than-life character who did something good for others.

2 A long time ago, there was a man who traveled across the country spreading apple seeds wherever he went. He was called Johnny Appleseed, and he's the reason there are so many apple trees in the country today.   USA

b. urban legend A recent, often frightening story about something that supposedly happened but probably didn't. Many people know the story and often think it's true.

3 A teenaged couple was sitting alone in a deserted spot when they heard on the radio about an escaped prisoner with a hook for a hand. They got scared and decided to leave, but before they could start the car, they heard a scraping sound on the door. They drove away quickly, and when they got home, they discovered a hook hanging from the car door.   USA

c. folktale An anonymous story about an imaginary character or event that is passed down orally from generation to generation.

4 A boy named Saci-Pererê lives in the forest. He has one leg and always wears a red hat. He comes out of the forest at night simply to scare people.   Brazil

d. myth An ancient story that most often describes the origin of something or a phenomenon of nature.

B Pair work Can you give at least one other example of each kind of story? Share your examples with the class.

listening **A** Listen to Marina and Frank tell stories. Take notes as you listen.

B Now take turns telling one of the stories in your own words.

reading **A** **Pair work** Discuss these questions with a partner. Then read the article, and compare your ideas with the author's.

1. Did you ever have the feeling that something terrible was going to happen?
2. Did you ever cancel any plans because something "inside you" made you feel uneasy?
3. Do you think that some people can predict the future?

The Sinking of the TITANIC

People sometimes have the feeling that they know something is going to happen. This is called a premonition. Some premonitions take the form of dreams or visions. Others are just strong feelings, ideas, or guesses that come into people's minds for no apparent reason.

Some people claim that they have premonitions at one time or another, but people known as psychics or clairvoyants appear to be more sensitive to whatever causes accurate premonitions. The following story is about the *Titanic* and the many apparently mysterious forewarnings that were reported.

In the early morning of April 15, 1912, the *Titanic*, the world's largest ocean liner at the time, struck an iceberg and sank on her maiden voyage across the Atlantic. A total of 1,502 lives were lost. Later investigation turned up at least 20 cases of people having premonitions of the disaster.

One of the strangest examples of an apparent premonition involved a novel called *Futility*, written in 1898 by Morgan Robertson. In the book, a huge liner, the *Titan*, sank after hitting an iceberg. Like the *Titanic*, the *Titan* was said to be unsinkable. Also like the *Titanic*, the *Titan* carried too few lifeboats for the large number of passengers on board.

In addition, there were two other stories that appeared to foretell the disaster, both written by a passenger on the doomed ship – one of them over 20 years earlier.

At least nine people had dreams in which a ship like the *Titanic* hit an iceberg and sank. Two clairvoyants gave warnings about the disaster, and several other people had extremely strong intuitions that something would go wrong. Some would-be passengers were so uneasy about the voyage that they canceled their tickets at the last minute. All these uncanny coincidences appear to be premonitions. There seems to be no way of explaining them.

Source: *Supernatural Guides: Mysterious Powers and Strange Forces*

B **Group work** Discuss these questions. Then share your answers with the class.

1. Why do you think so many people had premonitions about the *Titanic*?
2. Have you ever heard someone making predictions for the new year or about an important event? What was your opinion about those predictions?

Trends in reading

 What America reads

starting point **A** Read these statistics about reading in the United States. Where do you fit in?

Reading Preferences in the United States . . .

Top categories of popular adult books in the U.S. (% of total sales in 1998)		Some other facts . . .	
popular fiction	51.9%	55%	of people under 30 read newspapers
cooking/crafts	10.1%	38%	buy at least one magazine per month
religious	9.9%	27%	read at least one novel per year
general nonfiction	8.2%	16%	publicly claim to enjoy tabloids
psychology/recovery	6.3%		
technical/science/education	5.8%		
art/literature/poetry	3.9%		

Sources: American Book Association; *Kidbits* by Jenny Tesar

B Group work Discuss these questions and share your opinions with the class.

1. What do you read most frequently? What do you like to read most?
2. Do you buy many books? What kind? What have you purchased most recently?
3. Where do you buy your books? Why?
4. Do you use a library? What for?
5. Do you subscribe to any newspapers or magazines?
6. What do you think are the most popular categories of books in your country?

 The joys of literature

listening **A** Pair work In what ways do you think people benefit from reading literature such as novels, short stories, poetry, and plays? Make a list and share it with the class.

B 🔊 Listen to Junko and Andy discuss what people learn from reading literature. Make a list of the main points they make. Did you come up with similar points?

3 **Is it worth reading?**

discussion Group work Read what some college students have to say about reading. Do you agree with them? Give reasons. Discuss your opinions with the group.

"Obviously everything you find in a book you can learn from TV and the movies, so reading books is a waste of time."

"The Internet and electronic books could potentially lead to the end of printed books as we know them."

"Apparently comic books are a good way of getting children interested in reading."

"Supposedly the best way to study for a literature exam is not to read the novels but rather to study the summaries they sell in bookstores."

grammar
focus

Sentence adverbs

Sentence adverbs modify a whole sentence. Many of them express the attitude of the speaker.

Certainty: *clearly, obviously, unquestionably*
The Internet is **clearly** an important new means of communication.

Less certainty: *apparently, reportedly, supposedly*
Some companies **apparently** offer quality phone service over the Internet.

Possibility: *possibly, potentially, probably*
The Internet could **possibly** replace traditional long-distance telephone service.

Other attitudes: *not surprisingly, predictably, unfortunately*
Progress in communication **not surprisingly** has made life more efficient.
It has **unfortunately** made life more stressful as well.

Many sentence adverbs can occur at the beginning of the sentence as well as before or after the verb *be* and the auxiliaries *have* or *had*. *Clearly, obviously, apparently, supposedly, reportedly, predictably, not surprisingly,* and *unfortunately* all commonly appear at the beginning of a sentence.

Clearly the Internet is an important new means of communication.
The Internet **clearly** is an important new means of communication.
The Internet is **clearly** an important new means of communication.

Pair work Rewrite each sentence using one of the adverbs from the grammar box above. Place a sentence adverb at the beginning of at least four sentences. Compare with a partner.

1. Many writers claim that people nowadays rarely read serious literature.

   Supposedly people nowadays rarely read serious literature.

2. Publishers report that love stories are the biggest moneymakers among novels.
3. Many high school teachers claim that girls read more fiction than boys.
4. Some movie critics think that movies will eventually replace many forms of literature.
5. No one is surprised to hear that movies and TV have a bad effect on students' reading and writing skills.
6. It is obvious that reading is an important skill for using the Internet and that writing skills are essential for E-mail communication.
7. There's a chance that frequent use of the Internet could improve people's reading and writing skills.
8. Research shows that more people are literate now than ever before.
9. There's a good chance that paper will be so expensive in the future that books will become unaffordable.
10. It is possible that electronic books will replace paper books sooner than we think.

The future of reading

discussion **Group work** Discuss the statements you wrote above about trends in reading. When you are finished, make a list of four trends that you all agree will continue in the future.

A: Supposedly people nowadays rarely read serious literature. I guess that means that they only read romances and thrillers.
B: I don't think that people ever read much serious literature.
C: Well, I think more people read serious literature now than they did in the past. Apparently more people are literate now than ever before.

6 Books vs. the Internet

discussion **A** **Pair work** Look at these photographs, and discuss the questions.

computer room at the public library | reading room at the public library

1. What do you think each of these people is doing?
2. Which of these places would you be more likely to visit? Why?
3. What are some reasons you would choose one place over the other?

B **Group work** Read what these two people have to say about the advantages of books and the Internet. Who do you agree with? Why? Discuss the questions.

> "It's what I always wanted – to be in touch with a community of ideas like this. . . . There's something thrilling about the Internet. . . . It almost doesn't matter what anyone says. It's more the thrill of knowing you're in touch with people. . . ."
>
> – *Brian Eno, British rock musician*

> "I have fond childhood memories of being read to by my parents. I always looked forward to the bedtime stories, which sparked a love of reading that is still with me today. Although the Internet is a good source of information, it will never replace the creativity, imagination, and enrichment that books offer."
>
> – *Liane Golden, Student*

1. Do you use the Internet? How often and for what purposes?
2. How does the Internet affect your life?

7 Media growth

discussion **A** **Pair work** Look at the chart, and discuss the statistics with your partner.

1. Of all the media, which grew the most in the 1992–1997 period? Which ones decreased?
2. Do you think the information would be similar in your country?
3. Which category do you think has grown the most worldwide since 1997? What are your predictions for the next 20 years?

B **Group work** Summarize the advantages and disadvantages of using the Internet as compared to books, newspapers, and magazines. Share your answers with the class.

Consumer use of media in the U.S. 1992–1997

	1992	1997
	Average hours used per week	
Watching TV	29.0	31.0
Listening to the radio	22.1	21.0
Reading newspapers	3.3	3.0
Reading books	1.9	2.0
Reading magazines	1.6	1.7
Using the Internet	1.8	9.1

Source: "Who's on the Internet and Why," *The Futurist*

Writing a book report

A report on a novel generally answers the following questions:

1. What is the title of the book, and who is the author?
2. Who are the main characters?
3. Which character did you find most interesting? Why?
4. What is the story about? What is the central problem of the story, and how is it resolved?
5. Did you enjoy the book? Why or why not?
6. Would you recommend this book to another student? Why or why not?

A Read this book report. Find the answers to all of the questions in the box. Underline the answers.

The Incredible Journey

I recently read *The Incredible Journey* by Sheila Burnford, a book about three animal friends who travel across the Canadian wilderness looking for their owners. It is a fascinating story that describes some of the incredible things animals can do.

When a Canadian family goes to England for a long trip, they leave their three pets with a friend who lives 300 miles away. Though well treated by the friend, the pets miss their family. One day, they are able to leave the friend's house unnoticed and begin the long journey to find their owners. The central theme of the book, a problem the animals must resolve, is how to survive life in the wilderness in order to arrive home. They never could have completed the journey alone, but they take care of one another, and all three make it and are reunited with their owners.

The main characters in this book are a Siamese cat, an old English bullterrier, and a young Labrador retriever, the leader of the group. Each animal has a distinct personality, but they care for one another almost as if they were a family. My favorite of the three was the old bullterrier. Because of his age, the journey was the most difficult for him, but amazingly he found the strength to make it.

I liked the book very much. The author didn't try to turn the animals into people, speaking and acting like humans. Instead, she was faithful to their characters as animals and showed us their journey through animal eyes. That made the book both interesting and believable.

I would recommend the book to anyone who likes animals. Because most of the book focuses on the animals and contains little dialog, someone who is not interested in animals probably would not like the book. But I think that anyone who has ever had a pet or wanted a pet would enjoy it.

B Write a book report about a book you've read recently. Make sure your composition answers the questions in the box.

C Pair work Exchange your book report with a partner, and answer these questions.

1. Does your partner's book report answer all six questions? Find the answers.
2. Is the information in the report organized effectively? How could the organization be improved?
3. What other information about your partner's book would you like to know? Write at least one question.
4. Would you like to read the book your partner wrote about? Why or why not?

1 Choose a TV program

starting point

A Imagine you are looking at the TV listings, and these are the only TV programs available tonight. Which one would you most like to watch? Which one least interests you? Why?

Deep Sea

This week's program shows outstanding footage of divers swimming with killer sharks. Rarely has such amazing underwater photography been shown on TV.

Crime Watch

Detective Thomas is so involved in the investigation of the murder of a fellow police officer that he ignores the evidence that his wife is being stalked.

Rosie Adams

Today's show features interviews with people whose shopping habits have ruined their lives. Hardly ever has such an honest discussion of compulsive shopping been presented in a talk-show format.

B Pair work What are your favorite TV programs? What do you like about them?

2 Popular shows

vocabulary

A Look at these types of popular TV programs. Can you match each program with its description? Check your answers on page 118.

1. cartoon _f_
2. documentary ___
3. drama series ___
4. quiz show ___
5. sitcom (situation comedy) ___
6. soap opera ___
7. talk show ___

a. a continuing series, broadcast in some countries as often as five days a week, about the lives of a group of characters, often centering on their romantic lives
b. a program that gives biographical information about an interesting person, or factual information about a subject such as history, science, nature, or a social issue
c. a continuing series involving the same characters in various amusing situations
d. a show in which guests (sometimes celebrities or sometimes ordinary people involved in bizarre situations) are interviewed informally
e. a series, often shown weekly and frequently set in a hospital, police station, or law office, in which the same characters deal with frightening, emotional, or tragic situations
f. a film based on animated drawings, usually about a comical or adventurous situation
g. a program in which participants compete for money or prizes by answering questions, making guesses, or performing other tasks

B Pair work Can you name an example of five of the types of programs in Exercise A?

3 Negative adverbs at the beginning of a sentence

grammar focus

Negative adverbs of frequency (*never before, rarely, hardly ever,* and *seldom*) can be placed at the beginning of the sentence to give additional emphasis. This is more common in writing. Look at the sentences below. What happens to the subject and verb? When is *do* required?

Never before have viewers had so many TV channels to choose from. Nevertheless, it still can be difficult to find something worth watching.

Rarely do networks show nature documentaries on prime-time television. Those hours are reserved for dramas and sitcoms.

Hardly ever have sitcoms portrayed reality. They're meant to entertain viewers and make them laugh.

Rewrite these sentences placing negative adverbs at the beginning of a sentence. Discuss them with a partner. Which ones do you agree with?

1. Quiz shows seldom require participants to know a subject in any depth.

  Seldom do quiz shows require participants to know a subject in any depth.

2. Young people hardly ever watch soap operas. They can't relate to the stories or characters.
3. Political and social issues are rarely explored in depth on television.
4. News programs seldom report facts incorrectly.
5. Television rarely covers important world events except in a very superficial manner.

4 Such . . . that *and* so . . . that

grammar focus

You can express a result using the constructions *such . . . that, so . . . that, so much/little . . . that,* and *so many/few . . . that. Such* is followed by a noun (usually modified by an adjective), *so* by an adjective or adverb, *so many* and *so few* by countable nouns, and *so much* and *so little* by uncountable nouns.

Talk shows are **such *popular programs* that** almost every television network has at least one.
Talk shows are **so *popular* that** almost every television network has at least one.
There are **so many *different talk shows* that** it's impossible to watch them all.

Rewrite these sentences using *such . . . that* or *so . . . that*. Make any other necessary changes. Then compare with a partner.

1. Nature documentaries these days are incredibly well filmed. It is often hard to imagine how they took the shots.
2. Many TV programs show a lot of violence. People are becoming desensitized to it.
3. There are few good movies on TV these days. People are returning to movie theaters.
4. Television news reporting is very superficial. People are forced to get in-depth information elsewhere.
5. Sports broadcasts attract huge audiences. TV stations can charge large amounts for advertising.

5 Opinions about TV

discussion

Group work Complete these sentences with your own opinions, or write similar sentences. Then discuss them with your classmates.

"People watch so much television these days that . . ."

"Rarely do I watch TV late at night (in the morning, on Sundays, etc.) because . . ."

"There are so many different channels on TV now that . . ."

"Never before has television been so . . ."

listening   **A** Listen to these critics talk about some popular TV shows. In their opinion, why are the programs so successful?

	Reasons for success
Talk show	
Soap opera	
Sitcom	
Quiz show	

B   **Pair work**   Make a list of three popular TV shows, and discuss the reasons why these programs are so popular.

A: Many people like talk shows because guests are usually involved in the most bizarre situations.

B: Yes, but sometimes I doubt those situations are real. The other night, for example, I watched . . .

7   *Conflicting views on television*

discussion   **Group work**   Read these comments on the positive and negative influences of television. Which ones do you agree with? Add your own opinions. Then discuss in groups.

POSITIVE

☺ TV enables children with limited real-world experience to see how people around the world live and think.

☺ TV allows people to watch shows, musicals, and sports events that they might not be able to afford to watch live.

☺ TV brings the family together in a shared activity.

☺ TV is so appealing to children that parents don't have to be taking care of them all the time.

Your ideas: _____

NEGATIVE

☹ There is so much violence on TV that it encourages people to become violent.

☹ Children see many negative role models on TV, such as adults smoking or men mistreating women.

☹ Children develop a low attention span because they are overstimulated by TV.

☹ Advertising on TV turns people into compulsive shoppers.

☹ TV interferes with family life and communication. It's an intruder in the house.

Your ideas: _____

reading **A** Pair work Discuss these questions with a partner. Then read the article, and compare your ideas with the author's.

1. How much time do you spend in front of your TV set?
2. Are there any rules for watching TV in your house?

Tuning Out the TV

We were never TV addicts, but it was a central part of our lives, so I didn't know how my kids would react or what we would do when we first decided not to fix the television. The decision started as a financial one. It was going to cost more than we could afford to get the thing fixed.

Really, it was amazing how much the TV affected our lives. When the kids were being too noisy, I'd suggest they see what was on TV. Evening meals and social plans got scheduled around favorite TV shows. Conversations would suddenly get interrupted when someone said, "Hey, it's time for . . ." And recently I'd noticed that my kids weren't as well behaved as they used to be. I wondered if this might be partially the result of them attempting to imitate attitudes they saw on the tube. So I decided to experiment. We wouldn't fix the TV – for a week. After that, we'd see how it went. I was almost afraid to tell the kids, and when I did, their reaction was not exactly positive. They rolled their eyes as if to say, "Another one of her stupid ideas." Then they asked, "How about Nintendo®?" "Nope," I said. "And videos?" they asked. "None," I said. "How about movies in the movie theater?" asked my oldest. "Yes," I said, and they were relieved to have gotten at least that much.

The first day without TV was the worst – simply because I didn't know how it would go.

Worse than anything else was the fear and anticipation of life without television. I didn't have any problem, but I feared the kids would when they got home from school. I needn't have worried. They arrived home, looked at the broken TV, and went off to do something else. David practiced the piano for a while. Lisa looked through some magazines. Then they began playing together – something I hadn't seen happen in a while. And that evening, we actually talked at dinner. The evening went by quickly. We talked, listened to music, read – normal things. Life went on and it continues to go on.

The weeks passed and became two weeks. Now it's been a month. Today we removed the dead TV and took it out to the garage. No one really noticed. We get our news from the daily paper, magazines, and radio. When we want to, we go out to a movie. Instead of watching game shows, we play games. Rather than listen to other people talk about the issues of the day, we talk about them ourselves. The kids miss Nintendo® and some of their old favorite shows, mostly when other kids at school talk about them, but they seem to be surviving. They've developed other interests. We have, too. It's amazing how much more time we have now. Life without TV hasn't turned us into better people, but it's given us more of a chance to try.

B Group work Discuss these questions and share your ideas with the class.

1. What do you think are the advantages and disadvantages of the family's decision?
2. Have you ever gone without TV for a while? How did it affect you?
3. Do you think you could live without TV? How would your life be different?
4. Make a list of five ways in which you think you would be better off without TV and five ways in which you might be worse off. Share your answers with the class.

Lesson A *The enjoyment of art*

1 Art styles

starting point Look at these works of art, and read the comments people made about them. Can you match the comments and the paintings? Do you agree with the comments?

 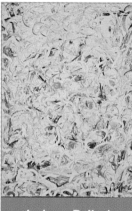  

| **Vincent van Gogh** *The Stroll, Evening* | **Jackson Pollock** *Shimmering Substance* | **Fernando Botero** *Head* | **Mary Cassatt** *Susan on a Balcony Holding a Dog* |

(1) "The more subtle the color combination in a painting, the more I enjoy looking at it."

(2) "This is original and eye-catching. I like the way the artist exaggerates reality to produce a sort of caricature."

(3) "I like this because for me art doesn't have to be a representation of reality. The less realistic a painting is, the more it fascinates me."

(4) "I like paintings that are easy to understand. I don't like having to figure out what things mean."

(5) "This isn't art to me because it doesn't show anything real. Anyone with a few cans of paint can do something like this."

(6) "I find this style very powerful. I like the way the artist uses broad brush strokes and vibrant colors."

2 Art preferences

discussion **A** **Pair work** Which of the above works of art do you like best? Which do you like least? Why? Have you seen any other works by these artists?

B **Group work** Join another pair and use the appropriate words below to describe the works of art in Exercise 1. Then discuss the questions.

painting / sculpture   landscape / portrait / still life   realistic / abstract

1. Do you prefer realistic art or abstract art? Why?
2. What kind of art do you like the most? Do you prefer paintings, sculpture, pottery, photography, or some other kind of art? Do you have a favorite artist?
3. Would you use a reproduction of any of the pieces of art on this page to decorate your home? Why? What other types of art might you use to decorate your home?

grammar focus

3 Double comparatives

To show that one quality or amount of something is linked to another quality or amount, use two comparatives, each preceded by *the*. In double comparatives, the first clause expresses a condition for the second clause.

The less realistic a painting (is), **the more** it fascinates me.
The more subtle the color combination in a painting, **the more** I enjoy looking at it.
The more realistic a painting (is), **the more quickly** it sells in an art gallery.
The more you learn about art, **the more** you appreciate it.
If you want to teach children to appreciate art, **the earlier** you start, **the better**.

A **Pair work** Match the clauses to make logical statements. Then compare with a partner. Which statements do you agree with? More than one answer may be possible.

1. The more you know about art, _c_
2. The more time you spend in art museums, ___
3. The more you know about the way an artist works, ___
4. The more art you put on your walls, ___
5. The less emphasis schools place on art, ___

a. the less creative the students become.
b. the more you realize how art can create a better living environment.
c. the more you are likely to enjoy looking at paintings.
d. the better you are able to appreciate different styles of art.
e. the better you will be able to understand his or her work.

> *I agree with the first statement. The more you know about something, the more interesting it is.*

B Complete these sentences with your own ideas. Can you add further information to clarify or support the statements you wrote?

1. The earlier children learn about art, . . .
2. The more realistic a work of art is, . . .
3. The longer I spend in an art museum, . . .
4. The more I see abstract art, . . .
5. The harder I try to draw something accurately, . . .
6. The older I get, . . .

C **Pair work** Compare and discuss the sentences you wrote in Exercise B. Share your opinions with the class.

> *The earlier children learn about art, the better, because learning about art helps with other subjects in school.*

> *I agree. I think that sometimes we just think of math or language as the important subjects, but in fact, . . .*

4   *Describing art*

vocabulary   **A**   These words are used to describe art. Can you match each with its definition? Check your answers on page 118.

1. abstract art __c__   3. impressionism ____   5. surrealism ____
2. cubism ____   4. pop art ____

   a. modern art movement that originated in the 1920s and 1930s. Objects are shown out of their normal context or as being made of inappropriate material. Humor, the world of dreams, and "the absurd" are three important themes of this movement.

   b. art movement that started in the early 1900s. Objects are painted in somber colors, like brown or gray, and are broken down into geometric shapes and planes, with several views depicted simultaneously.

   c. form of art in which there is no attempt to represent objects or people, but which relies totally on lines, colors, and shapes

   d. form of art that developed in the 1960s based on aspects of twentieth-century life such as movies, advertising, comics, and everyday products

   e. art movement that started in France in the 1860s. The artists use bright colors, and they try to capture the effects of sunlight on water, trees, and fields.

B   **Pair work**   Use the concepts in Exercise A to classify these paintings. Do you know other examples of each style?

Andy Warhol
Twenty Marilyns

Salvador Dalí
Untitled

Pablo Picasso
Weeping Woman

5   *Let's meet Andy Warhol.*

listening   💿   Listen to a talk about the American artist Andy Warhol. When was he born? What style of art did he pioneer? What are his most famous works?

6   *Famous artists*

discussion   **Class activity**   Prepare a short class presentation about a famous artist from your country. What style(s) of art is he or she known for? What's your opinion of his or her work? Where can you see examples of his or her art?

> One of the most famous modern artists in Mexico is Diego Rivera. He is most famous for his mural paintings; many of them are about the Mexican Revolution and the life of the Mexican people. You can see his work in many public buildings, especially in the National Palace in Mexico City.

Classification essay

writing

A classification essay organizes information into classes or categories. The first paragraph offers an overview of the categories. Each subsequent paragraph provides information about a single category. A conclusion summarizes the information presented and gives an additional perspective on the overall topic.

A Read this draft of an essay. Identify the different parts described in the box above.

> Three of the major painting styles represented in many art museums are romanticism, impressionism, and abstract art. Though very different from one another, these three styles represent some of the major achievements in Western art from the nineteenth century up to the present time.
>
> Romanticism was prominent in the first half of the nineteenth century, reaching its peak in France in the 1830s. Romantic artists chose highly emotional subjects for their art such as death, disasters, . . .
>
> Impressionism refers to a late nineteenth-century style developed by French painters who tried to capture the brilliant effect of sunlight on colorful outdoor scenes. . . .
>
> Abstract art refers to nonrepresentational art of the twentieth century. This includes the geometric style of such painters as Kandinsky and Klee. . . .
>
> Although each style is unique, they are also related. Each style builds on the previous one and also reacts against it. . . .

B **Pair work** Plan a classification essay on a topic related to art such as museums or types of art in your city or country. First, make notes on the following topics:

1. How many different kinds of museums or art are there?
2. Choose three different types of museums or art, and for each one write down:
   a. what kind of museum or art it is
   b. what it contains or consists of
   c. what some of its special or distinguishing features are

C Write a classification essay that includes an introduction, three or more paragraphs – each about a different museum or type of art – and a conclusion.

D **Pair work** Read your partner's essay, looking at overall organization and content. What are its strengths and weaknesses?

Milestones of popular music

starting
point

A Look at these milestones in the history of popular music. How many of the singers and groups in the chart have you heard of? What else do you know about them?

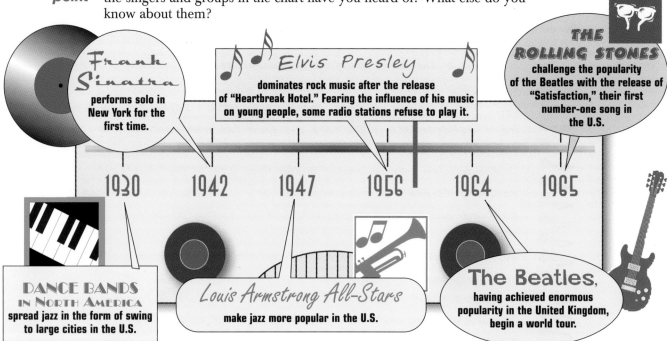

Frank Sinatra performs solo in New York for the first time.

Elvis Presley dominates rock music after the release of "Heartbreak Hotel." Fearing the influence of his music on young people, some radio stations refuse to play it.

THE ROLLING STONES challenge the popularity of the Beatles with the release of "Satisfaction," their first number-one song in the U.S.

1930   1942   1947   1956   1964   1965

DANCE BANDS IN NORTH AMERICA spread jazz in the form of swing to large cities in the U.S.

Louis Armstrong All-Stars make jazz more popular in the U.S.

The Beatles, having achieved enormous popularity in the United Kingdom, begin a world tour.

B Pair work Discuss these questions with a partner, and share the information with the class.

1. What are some musical milestones in your country?
2. What singers or groups are popular in your country now?

Musical styles

vocabulary

A Read these descriptions of different types of music. What type of music is each description about? Check your answers on page 118.

1. country and western _e_   3. jazz _____   5. rock 'n' roll _____
2. folk music _____   4. new age music _____

a. music of African-American origin with improvisation and a strong rhythm
b. popular music with a strong beat, usually played with electric guitars and drums
c. a soft, soothing form of instrumental music often used to promote relaxation
d. traditional songs often performed with simple instruments such as the banjo and guitar
e. music that is popular today in the U.S., especially in the Southern states. Often based on the music of cowboys in the American West, it is accompanied by a banjo, violin, or guitar.

B Pair work If you could attend a concert featuring one of the types of music above, which one would you choose? Which one would you be least interested in? Are there any other types of music you would prefer?

3

grammar focus

Cause and effect with participles

Causal relationships can be expressed by participles. The subject of both the main and the dependent clauses must be the same. Notice these patterns.

Action verbs: In most cases, clauses beginning with *because, since,* or *as* that contain action verbs are reduced by combining the present participle of *have* and the past participle of the main verb.

Because he **had listened** to African-American music while growing up, Elvis Presley incorporated many of its features into his music.

Having listened to African-American music while growing up, Elvis Presley incorporated many of its features into his music.

Nonaction or stative verbs: Stative (nonaction) verbs such as *be, have, fear, know, like, realize, think,* and *want* can be reduced by changing the verb to the present participle.

Because they **feared** the influence of Elvis Presley's music on young people, some radio stations refused to play it.

Fearing the influence of Elvis Presley's music on young people, some radio stations refused to play it.

However, if the verb in the first clause expresses a state or condition that began before the state or action expressed by the verb in the second clause, the verb is generally reduced by using the auxiliary *have.*

Because I have always **liked** the Beatles, I am thrilled that some radio stations still play their music.

Having always **liked** the Beatles, I am thrilled that some radio stations still play their music.

A Rewrite these sentences with participial phrases.

1. As he had become completely deaf, Beethoven was forced to compose music "in his head."

   Having become completely deaf, Beethoven was forced to compose music "in his head."

2. Since he wanted to avoid the public spotlight, former Beatle George Harrison withdrew to the country.
3. Because they realize the sales potential of the Internet, music producers have made samples of music available on-line.
4. Because he came from a steel-manufacturing town, Bruce Springsteen has written songs about working people and their dreams.
5. Since she had frequently performed for her family, Japanese violinist Midori was prepared to play her violin in front of large audiences when she was only eight years old.
6. Because she grew up exposed to both Cuban and American culture, Miami-based singer Gloria Estefan has been able to fuse these two cultures in her music.

B **Pair work** Rewrite these clauses with participial phrases. Then complete each sentence with your own information. Discuss with a partner.

1. Since music producers realize teenagers buy more music CDs than anybody else, . . .
2. Because parents worry about the effects of violent music lyrics, . . .
3. As most parents have different musical tastes from their children, . . .
4. Since I've always liked _____ music, . . .
5. Because I fear loud music will damage my hearing, . . .

4 The uses of music

discussion

A Pair work What kind of music would you expect to hear in these places? What purpose does music serve in each situation?

gym

supermarket

cafe

A: In a gym, you usually hear loud rock music with a fast beat.
B: I guess that's because . . .

B Group work What kinds of music do you usually hear in each of these situations? What purpose does music serve?

1. TV commercials   2. political rallies   3. sports events   4. movies

A: Have you noticed that TV commercials for luxury cars usually play classical music?
B: Yes, and they use pop music to advertise small cars. . . .

C Group work Can you think of some movies where music was used particularly well?

> One of the best examples I can think of is how the music was used in the movie "Jaws."
> When the shark is about to attack, the music starts slowly and then gets faster and faster.

5 Music helps the mind

listening

Listen to a talk about how music can help a person's mind. What are three positive effects of classical music?

Positive effects

reading **A** Pair work Should music education be mandatory in schools? List three reasons to support your opinion. Then read the article, and compare your ideas with the author's.

1. _____

2. _____

3. _____

We Study Music Because . . .

Researchers have shown that music has many uses besides recreation. Below is a list of reasons why some people believe music should be an important component of the school curriculum.

To study music is to study a basic form of communication. Music, like reading, writing, and speaking, conveys thoughts, ideas, and feelings. It is used for such mundane purposes as selling commercial products and for such noble purposes as inspiring and elevating our appreciation of life.

To study music is to study the world's peoples. Music is an important means of learning about and transmitting cultural heritages. Music helps us to learn about ourselves, our traditions, and our ways of thinking and acting. It also helps us to learn about others, their traditions, and their behaviors.

To study music is to study the learning process. Through music, people become engaged in the learning process and develop keener insights into how knowledge, skills, attitudes, feelings, and the senses interrelate.

To study music is to study the imagination and self-expression. Music provides an avenue for developing self-expression and creativity.

To study music is to study the basics. Music is a comprehensive art. Through its study, students come into contact with other basic areas of the curriculum: math, science, social studies, languages, and physical education.

To study music is to study art. Music offers us an opportunity to develop aesthetic sensitivity. The study of music teaches people to appreciate quality – those products of human creativity that represent the highest order of thinking, feeling, and technical achievement.

Source: "A Stronger Rationale for Music Education" by Kenneth H. Phillips, *Music Educators Journal*

B Group work Discuss these questions. Then share your answers with the class.

1. Which of the reasons for studying music listed in the article do you agree with most? Why?
2. Can you think of some practical uses of music in everyday life?

1 Reporting clauses

Complete these sentences with an appropriate verb. Then add a statement giving information of your own. Compare with a partner.

admit   assume   doubt   report
argue   claim   feel

1. Many people ___claim___ that they have no superstitious beliefs.
2. Some people _____ that certain colors are lucky for them.
3. Many people _____ that they follow astrology in the newspaper every day.
4. Some people _____ that superstitious beliefs influence their decisions.
5. Researchers _____ that superstitions are common in all cultures.
6. Most people _____ that good luck charms will protect them from harm.

> Many people claim that they have no superstitious beliefs. I feel that most people have a few superstitions.

> I admit that I have a few superstitions myself.

2 Reporting clauses in the passive

A Complete these sentences with an appropriate verb. Then rewrite each statement with a passive form of the verb and *it*. More than one tense may be possible.

argue   believe   estimate   report   suggest   think

1. Some research __has suggested__ that many people have had "out-of-body" experiences.

It has been suggested that many people have had "out-of-body" experiences.

2. Skeptics _____ that most UFO sightings are caused by unusual weather conditions.
3. People _____ that those who believe in aliens have lost touch with reality.
4. Some people _____ that scientists will eventually discover life on another planet.
5. Some specialists _____ that over half of adult Americans believe in ghosts.
6. Recent articles _____ that supernatural beliefs are on the increase.

B **Pair work** Work in pairs and ask each other's opinion about the statements in Exercise A.

A: It has been suggested that many people have had "out-of-body" experiences. What do you think?
B: I don't think that's true. Some people just like publicity. . . .

3   Negative adverbs at the beginning of a sentence

A   Rewrite these people's opinions about TV programs using negative adverbs at the beginning of a sentence.

1. Television rarely gives ordinary people the chance to express their views.

Rarely does television give ordinary people the chance to express their views.

2. Music videos hardly ever provide worthwhile artistic content.
3. People have never been so well informed as they are now, thanks to TV news programs.
4. TV documentaries rarely focus on the achievements of women.
5. Children's programs are seldom considered both educational and entertaining.

B   Pair work   Discuss the opinions in Exercise A with a partner. Which opinions do you agree with most? Why?

4   Such ... that *and* so ... that

Write sentences about these topics using *so . . . that* and *such . . . that.* Compare your ideas with a partner.

TV news programs   kids' TV shows   cooking shows   TV commercials   soap operas

TV news programs are so superficial that many people prefer reading the newspaper.

5   Double comparatives

Complete these statements with your own information. Then add a statement to strengthen or support your point of view. Share and discuss your ideas with a partner.

1. The sooner children realize the importance of art, . . .

The sooner children realize the importance of art, the more they'll enjoy art classes. . . .

2. The less money governments spend on the arts, . . .
3. The greater an artist's reputation becomes, . . .
4. The more artistic a person is, . . .
5. The more people study art history, . . .

6   Cause and effect with participles

A   Fill in the blanks with a kind of music. Then rewrite the clauses with participles, and complete each sentence with your own information.

1. Because I grew up listening to _____, . . .

Having grown up listening to classical music, I prefer it to all other kinds of music.

2. Since I've never appreciated _____, . . .
3. Because I hoped at one time to become a _____ musician, . . .
4. Since my parents have always preferred _____, . . .
5. Because I know my best friend loves _____, . . .

B   Pair work   Compare and discuss your ideas about music. Does your partner agree?

7

What a story!

A **Pair work** Read the beginning of these stories. Then add a possible ending, or think of a story of your own.

Some residents in rural New Mexico say that they hear a constant noise that is causing them health problems. It is reported that the noise probably comes from . . .

A woman in Washington reports that her phone rings up to 100 times a day. Normally there would be nothing very surprising about this, but the calls have continued even though the woman had her phone disconnected. It is believed that . . .

Residents of San Francisco say that they are often woken up by bright lights in the night. It is believed that the flashes of light are caused by low-flying aircraft. However, . . .

B **Pair work** Work with a student from a different pair. Take turns telling your story. Whose story is more believable?

You have to read this!

Group work Talk about your reading habits. Ask and answer follow-up questions about these topics.

- the book you would recommend the most
- the magazine or newspaper you like the most
- the most interesting character you've ever come across in a story you've read
- the magazine or newspaper you would never buy

A: The book I would recommend the most is . . .
B: What's it about?
A: It's about . . .
C: Why do you like it?
A: Because . . .

9 What kind of show is it?

A Think of an example of each type of show. For each show, write down two things you like about it and two things you'd like to change.

Type of show	Example	Comments
Quiz show		
Educational TV show		
Drama series		
Music show		
Talk show		

B Group work   Compare and discuss your ideas.

> Rarely have I seen a quiz show as boring as . . .

> Oh, really? I find it kind of informative. You can learn a lot from watching it.

10 Art opinions

Pair work   Do you agree with these statements about art? Can you add two more statements to the list? Compare answers with a partner, and ask follow-up questions.

	Agree	Disagree
1. Painting is a learned skill, and even people without any special talent can learn to paint.	☐	☐
2. No good art has been produced in the last 50 years.	☐	☐
3. Art improves the quality of people's lives.	☐	☐
4. Artists should receive a salary from the government until they are established.	☐	☐
5. More art should be put in public places.	☐	☐
6. Abstract paintings are not real art.	☐	☐
7. _____		
8. _____		

A: I agree with the first one. There are many things you can learn to do if you just work at them.
B: I see your point, but obviously good artists have a natural talent that we don't all share.

11 Hit songs

Group work   In your opinion, what are the five best songs of all time? Make a list that you all agree on. Then share your ideas with the class.

> Probably the best song of all time is . . .

> Well, it was very popular, but . . .

Lesson A   *Lifestyles in transition*

1   How we are changing

starting point

A   People's lifestyles are changing more quickly than ever before. Are any of the changes below occurring in your country?

1. Eating healthful foods and getting regular exercise have become important to both younger and older people.

2. Increasingly, parents who are disappointed with the quality of education in traditional institutions are deciding to educate their children at home.

3. Many professionals who used to commute to their jobs are now working from home.

4. Medical therapies that use herbs, natural oils, and other techniques are becoming more widespread.

5. Many people are accepting jobs with fewer responsibilities and lower salaries because they want to live a less stressful life.

6. Many people are choosing to eat foods that are not derived from animals.

7. People who want to develop muscular bodies are joining gyms and health clubs.

B   Pair work   List three other ways in which lifestyles are changing in your country. Share your ideas with the class.

> I think young people are much less traditional and more individualistic than they were even ten years ago. They don't worry so much about what others think of them.

2   New trends

vocabulary

Pair work   These expressions refer to current trends affecting people's customs and lifestyles. Match each expression to a statement from Exercise A above. Which of these trends do you think are most beneficial?

a. alternative medicine _4_
b. bodybuilding___
c. fitness___

d. homeschooling___
e. telecommuting___

f. vegetarianism___
g. voluntary simplicity___

Relative pronouns in defining relative clauses

A number of different relative pronouns are used to introduce defining relative clauses. When the relative pronoun is the subject of the clause, it is required. When it is the object, it is usually optional.

Relative pronouns referring to people

Subject of clause (required): Professionals **who/that** used to commute to their jobs are now working from home.

Object of clause (optional): An herbal therapist is a health professional **(who/that/whom)** more and more people are consulting about both mental and physical health.

Relative pronouns referring to things

Subject of clause (required): People are demanding vegetables and fruits **that/which** have been grown without the use of chemicals.

Object of clause (optional): Herbal therapy is an option **(that/which)** more and more people are considering as an alternative to traditional medicine.

Relative pronouns as objects of prepositions

In colloquial English, relative pronouns that are the objects of prepositions are optional. In more formal language, however, the preposition generally precedes the relative pronoun and either *which* or *whom* must be used.

Optional: My herbal therapist is the health professional **(who/that/whom)** I speak to most often.
Insomnia is a problem **(that/which)** herbal therapy is commonly used for.

Required: My herbal therapist is the health professional to **whom** I speak most often.
Insomnia is a problem for **which** herbal therapy is commonly used.

Relative pronouns referring to possession

Required: Parents **whose** children are not doing well in traditional schools are turning to homeschooling as a solution.

A Check the sentences in which the relative pronoun is optional. How many sentences are true in your community? Can you think of a specific example for each?

1. A lot of people who have grown tired of city life are moving to the country.
2. People who use the Internet join chat groups to socialize.
3. E-mail is an efficient form of communication that many businesses rely on.
4. People are devoting more time to others who are less fortunate.
5. People are recycling many of the things which they would normally have thrown away in the past.

B Fill in the blanks with *who, whom, whose, that,* or *which.*

1. Is life becoming easier or more difficult for couples ___*who/that*___ live together without getting married?
2. Are problems _____ arise nowadays between couples different from or the same as problems _____ couples had in the past?
3. Is it wrong for women _____ have children to work outside the home?
4. Are there any household chores for _____ men are better suited than women or vice versa?
5. Should men _____ wives have better-paying jobs stay at home and take care of the children?

C Pair work Interview each other using the questions in Exercise B. Ask and answer follow-up questions.

It's a matter of choice.

discussion **A** Pair work Read this information about the lifestyle that Alice has chosen. Make a list of the advantages and disadvantages of Alice's choice.

Alice Bain, a 36-year-old woman from Seattle, is typical of many people these days. She is happily married, enjoys her job, has lots of friends, and spends the weekends doing exactly what she wants. She has it all. The only thing she doesn't have is children – and she doesn't want any. Family members ask when, not if, she is going to have a baby. But Alice isn't thinking about motherhood. "Kids are fine," she says. "It's just that taking care of another human being is not what I want to be doing with my life for the next 20 years."

B Group work Join another pair and discuss your ideas. Do more people agree or disagree with Alice's choice?

A: One advantage is that she would have more time for herself if she doesn't have kids.
B: Yes, but I don't think her life will be very fulfilling. It seems like a very selfish choice.
C: I don't think you need to have children to live a fulfilling life. . . .

 Life choices

discussion **A** Pair work Discuss the situations below. What are the advantages and disadvantages of each? Would you do something similar to what these people did? Why or why not?

> Silvia gave up a successful and well-paid career as a lawyer to become a kindergarten teacher.

> Doug sold his apartment in the city to move to a suburban house so he could telecommute and do his work at home.

> Hiroshi turned down a job at a bank in order to work as a volunteer for a disaster relief organization.

B Pair work Imagine you are one of the people above. Take turns interviewing each other to find out why they made the choice they did.

 Generation gap

listening Listen to Chris's and Paula's opinions on differences between their generation and that of their parents, and complete the chart.

Difference	Is the difference positive?

writing

A composition about a personal experience usually begins with an introductory paragraph containing a thesis statement and some observations or comments. The body of the composition provides background information and gives details about what happened. The conclusion usually restates the thesis and presents the writer's feelings.

A Underline the thesis statement. Then answer the questions, and compare answers with a partner.

> Last month I took a giant step and finally moved to a new apartment. I had been sharing a two-bedroom apartment with a friend for the last two years and decided that it was time to have my own place. In the beginning, I was a little scared because I would be assuming a great deal of financial responsibility. I was also a little concerned about feeling lonely, but I knew that I wanted to have the experience of being totally on my own.
>
> The first thing I wanted to do before making a final decision was to talk things over with my roommate. We had first moved in together because neither of us could afford . . .
>
> I looked at many apartments before making up my mind. I finally found an affordable studio in very good shape, with a lot of light. The apartment is . . .
>
> My apartment now is beginning to look like a home. I've been looking at a lot of interior design magazines, and I managed to decorate my apartment. . . .
>
> I really feel good about having a place I can call my own. Sometimes I feel a little lonely, but for the most part I enjoy the privacy. . . .

1. What observations or personal comments does the writer make in the first paragraph?
2. What kinds of details does the body of the composition provide?

B Write a composition about something that has happened to you recently. Make sure to include an introductory paragraph, three paragraphs with details, and a conclusion.

C Pair work Exchange papers and answer these questions.

1. Does your partner's introductory paragraph have a thesis statement?
2. Do all the details in the body of the composition support the thesis statement?
3. What other points or examples could be added?

Lesson B *Setting goals*

1   *Taking stock*

starting point

A Read what these people say about themselves. Who is most like you? Who is least like you?

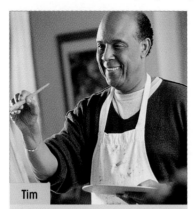

Tim

"Spending time alone doesn't bother me as it did when I was younger. I enjoy doing things on my own, and I don't need company all the time."

Rebecca

"I feel as though there is never enough time in the day to do all the things I need to do. I wish I knew how to use time more effectively."

Scott

"I would like to spend more time just having fun, the way most of my friends do. I really need more fun in my life."

B   **Pair work**   In which of these areas do you think you could use some improvement? Rank your priorities from 1 (most important) to 6 (least important). Then discuss your answers.

____ developing new friendships   ____ getting more exercise   ____ saving money
____ expressing yourself   ____ learning to relax   ____ managing time

> *The most important thing for me right now is to save some money. I want . . .*

C   **Group work**   Look back at your life over the last few years, and discuss these questions.

1. Have you achieved some of your long-term goals? Which ones?
2. What goals are you working on now?
3. What are some of the most valuable things you've learned?
4. What are some things you still want to learn?
5. Has anything happened that has changed your life in an important way?

2   *Goal achievers*

listening

 Listen to three people describing goals they set for themselves and how they achieved them. Complete the chart.

	Goals	How they achieved them
Charles		
Melissa		
Brian		

3

grammar focus

As if, as though, as, the way, *and* like

As if and *as though* often introduce clauses that describe behavior or feelings.
I feel **as if/as though** there is never enough time in the day.
My brother sometimes acts **as if/as though** he's totally crazy.

As and *the way* introduce clauses that express a comparison.
Spending time alone doesn't bother me **as/the way** it did when I was younger.

In colloquial English, the word *like* can be substituted for *as if/as though* and *as/the way*.
I feel **like** there is never enough time in the day.
Spending time alone doesn't bother me **like** it did when I was younger.

A Pair work Rewrite these sentences to make them more formal using *as if, as though, as,* or *the way*. Compare your answers with a partner.

1. I need to work on my communication skills because sometimes I feel like I'm not getting my message across.

   I need to work on my communication skills because sometimes I feel as if I'm not getting my message across.

2. I like to work by myself so that I don't feel like I'm being pushed around by anybody.
3. Lately, I'm trying to spend more time with my family and friends like I did before I got involved in so many other activities.
4. I have to establish more realistic goals like my career advisor has suggested.
5. These days, women are not expected to stay at home like their mothers did in the past.
6. Sometimes I feel like I'm not doing enough exercise and I spend too much time sitting at a desk.

B Pair work Complete these sentences so that they are true for you. Add two more sentences with your own information, and compare with a partner.

1. I feel as if . . .

   I feel as if I need a long vacation.

2. I don't need to be with people all the time as . . .
3. I feel as though I never have enough time to . . .
4. I would like to spend more time with my friends the way . . .
5. I still enjoy swimming just like . . .
6. _____
7. _____

C Group work Join another pair and share your information. Comment and give each other advice.

A: I really feel as if I need a long vacation.
B: Have you been under a lot of stress lately?
   You look as though . . .
A: It's been awful. I've been working around the clock.
C: Well, I think . . .

discussion **A** Pair work List three of your short-term and three of your long-term goals, and share them with your partner. Do you think you are likely to achieve them? Why or why not?

A: I want to retire by the time I'm 40.
B: Is that realistic? How are you going to manage that?
A: Well, if I start planning now . . .

B Pair work Read these suggestions on how to achieve your personal goals. Check the suggestions you find helpful, and add two more of your own. Which ones will help you achieve the goals you discussed in Exercise A?

☐ Set short-term and long-term goals that you can realistically achieve.
☐ Make a step-by-step list of the things you will have to do to achieve your goals.
☐ Identify possible obstacles and make a plan for overcoming each one.
☐ Talk about your goals with others.
☐ Monitor yourself regularly to see if you are on target.
☐ Reward yourself whenever you achieve a goal.
☐ _____
☐ _____

discussion Group work Now apply the ideas you discussed in Exercises A and B to these situations. What advice would you give these people?

Luis is leaving next month to spend a year in a foreign country and needs a working knowlege of the language spoken there.

Kelly wants to have enough money to pay a credit card balance that is presently equal to three months of her salary.

Emily wants to change careers. She is an accountant and now wants to become a freelance photographer.

Luis needs to be realistic about learning a foreign language in such a short time. He should begin by setting a possible short-term goal. . . .

reading **A** Pair work Discuss these questions with a partner. Then read the article, and compare your ideas with the ones described in it.

1. Do you think people would be better off reducing their income in half in exchange for more free time and less stress?
2. Name three things you would be willing to spend less money on and three areas where you would have a hard time cutting expenses.

More People Are Leaving the Rat Race for the Simple Life

Time is more precious than money for an increasing number of people who are choosing to live more with less – and liking it.

Kay and Charles Giddens, a paralegal and a trial lawyer, respectively, sold their home to start a bed and breakfast. Four years later, the couple dishes out banana pancake breakfasts, cleans toilets, serves homemade chocolate chip cookies to guests in a bed and breakfast surrounded by trees on a mesa known for colorful sunsets.

"Do I miss the freeways? Do I miss the traffic? Do I miss the stress? No," says Ms. Giddens. "This is a phenomenon that's fairly widespread. A lot of people are reevaluating their lives and figuring out what they want to do. If their base is eroding on them, what's the payoff?"

Simple living ranges from cutting down on weeknight activities to sharing housing, living closer to work and commuting less, avoiding shopping malls, borrowing books from the library instead of buying them, and taking a cut in pay to work at a more pleasurable job.

Vicki Robin, a writer, lives on a budget equivalent to a fifth of what she used to make.

"You become conscious about where your money is going and how valuable it is," Ms. Robin says. "You tend not to use things up. You cook at home rather than eat out. Your life is less frantic, and you discover your expenses have gone way down. People are very interested in how they can save money and how they can get out of debt."

Janet Luhrs, a lawyer, quit her practice after giving birth and leaving her daughter with a nanny for two weeks. "It was not the way I wanted to raise my kids," she says. "Simplicity is not just about saving money, it's about me sitting down every night with my kids to a candlelit dinner with classical music."

Mrs. Luhrs now edits a magazine, *Simple Living*, which publishes tips on how to buy recycled furniture and shoes, organize potluck dinners instead of fancy receptions, and generally how to consume less.

"It's not about poverty or deprivation," Mrs. Luhrs explains. "It's about conscious living and creating the life you want. The less stuff you buy, the less money goes out the door, and the less money you have to earn."

Source: "More People Are Leaving the Rat Race for the Simple Life"
by Julia Duin, *The Washington Times*

B Group work Discuss these questions. Then share your answers with the class.

1. Can you summarize the main idea of the article in one or two sentences?
2. Do you think the lives of the people portrayed in the article have improved as a result of their decisions? Why or why not?
3. Would you be willing to adopt a form of voluntary simplicity? Why?

What's new on the market?

1 New products

starting point

A Pair work Look at these new products and services, and discuss the questions.

Bouncing boots

A sports shoe called the "Bouncing Boot" allows humans to jump like kangaroos. People wearing these boots can make powerful leaps and landings without injury. The shoes can also be used by people with walking difficulties.

E-mail with your coffee

Some convenience stores are offering their customers a new service. When customers pick up coffee or a sandwich, they will also be able to check their E-mail in the store.

Computerized books

Software stores are recommending a new product to their customers. You can now buy a whole book on a disk that fits into a handheld reader with an adjustable screen.

1. Which of the above products or services do you think are likely to be successful or unsuccessful? Why?
2. Who do you think would be most likely to buy or use them?
3. Would you consider using any of these products or services? Which ones?

B Group work Can you think of any successful products manufactured in your city or country? Why are they successful?

2 To buy or not to buy?

listening

  Listen to sales representatives describing new products. Are these products selling well? Complete the chart.

Product	Is it selling well?	Why or why not?

Placement of direct and indirect objects

For most verbs in English, including *give, lend, mail, send, show, teach,* and *tell,* direct and indirect objects follow these patterns:

Pattern A
direct object + *to* + indirect object
The store mailed **the boots to John.**
The store mailed **the boots to him.**
The store mailed **them to John.**
The store mailed **them to him.**

Pattern B
indirect object + direct object
The store mailed **John the boots.**
The store mailed **him the boots.**

With verbs such as *announce, describe, explain, mention, recommend, return,* and *say,* the indirect object cannot precede the direct object. Sentences follow pattern A above.

direct object + *to* + indirect object
They explained **the new product (it) to their customers (them).**

With verbs such as *allow, ask, cause,* and *cost,* the indirect object generally precedes the direct object and takes no preposition. Sentences follow pattern B above.

indirect object + direct object
The boots cost **John (him) a hundred dollars.**
John asked **the store (them) several questions** about his bill.

A Complete these sentences using the words in parentheses. Whenever possible, write the sentence in two different ways.

1. Companies want to get customers to try their new products, so they send . . . (free samples/them)

   Companies want to get customers to try their new products, so they send them free samples.

   Companies want to get customers to try their new products, so they send free samples to them.

2. I bought a great new CD player at a very reasonable price, so I recommended . . . (it/my friends)
3. Some cafes look for innovative ways to attract new business. Many of them offer . . . (E-mail service/their customers)
4. When I'm shopping, I always look for friendly and knowledgeable salesclerks. That way I can ask . . . (many questions/them)
5. Good salespeople are able to explain . . . (all the benefits of a product/their customers)
6. I never keep something I've purchased if I'm not fully satisfied. I always return . . . (defective merchandise/the refund department)

B Pair work Use the verbs below to talk about the things you've bought recently. Ask and answer follow-up questions.

ask	describe	give	return
cost	explain	recommend	tell

A: Last week I bought a pair of in-line skates. They cost me a fortune.
B: Why did you get them?
A: Well, I heard about a new model that's specially made for jumping.
B: Do you really need such fancy skates?
A: Actually, I don't. I'm thinking of returning them to the store.

vocabulary **A** Pair work Match each expression with its meaning. Then compare with a partner.

1. bargain hunters *f*
2. price war ____
3. black market ____
4. window-shopping ____
5. shopping spree ____
6. compulsive shoppers ____

a. illegal trading to avoid regulations or taxes
b. competition between businesses to offer the lowest price
c. people who have an uncontrollable need to buy things
d. shopping trip where you buy a lot of expensive things
e. looking at goods without purchasing anything
f. people who are always looking for low-priced goods

B Pair work Write a sentence, either positive or negative, about each expression in Exercise A. Then compare with a partner.

Positive: A successful bargain hunter can often save a lot of money on clothes, household items, and groceries.
Negative: Bargain hunters take five times as long to do their shopping.

C Group work Discuss your own recent shopping experiences. Use the vocabulary in Exercise A where appropriate.

A: I went on a shopping spree yesterday. I bought three pairs of shoes.
B: Three pairs! You must have spent a lot of money.

discussion **A** Pair work Which statements are true about you? Check yes or no for each statement, and discuss it with a partner.

	Yes	No
1. When the latest clothing styles are in the stores, I have to buy them.	☐	☐
2. I often buy things that I find I never use.	☐	☐
3. I sometimes shop in order to forget my troubles.	☐	☐
4. When I visit a new city, I spend most of the time shopping.	☐	☐
5. I feel guilty after going on a shopping spree.	☐	☐
6. I have a difficult time paying my credit card bills.	☐	☐
7. I can't go window-shopping without buying something.	☐	☐
8. I've lied to relatives or friends about the prices of things I've bought.	☐	☐

B Group work Discuss these questions and share your ideas with the class.

1. What are some other characteristics of a compulsive shopper?
2. What other problems do compulsive shoppers face?
3. What would you tell a compulsive shopper to help him or her control the urge to buy things?

writing

> When writing a composition that supports an opinion, first present the opinion in the thesis statement. Then support it in subsequent paragraphs with examples and details.

A   Read the composition and discuss the questions.

1. What is the writer's opinion?
2. What are the reasons given to support the opinion?

> Because credit cards present many advantages, they have become widespread. However, the use of credit cards also causes problems. Many people run up such high debts that they go bankrupt, creating problems for their families as well as for the people to whom they owe money. I think there should be a limit to the amount of credit people can have. This way, the total amount of credit on all of their credit cards together could never go over a certain percentage of their income.
>
> With unlimited credit, people spend too much money. Currently, it is easy for people to accumulate many credit cards. Although the credit cards have limits, the number of credit cards is not limited. People with ten credit cards, each with a $5,000 limit, have $50,000 of credit, even though they might not be able to pay all of their bills. Such a situation can quickly lead to bankruptcy.
>
> People need to be given an absolute credit limit. If people were not permitted to go over this limit, they would have to be more responsible with their money and evaluate which purchases were most important to them. I think that the actual limit on credit card spending should be based on income so that credit would be based on the ability to pay.

B   Complete one of these opinions on shopping. Then present your opinion in a thesis statement.

1. No one under 21 should be allowed to . . .
2. Businesses should give preferred customers . . .
3. Stores should never give cash refunds for . . .
4. Customers who break an item in a store should . . .
5. Shoplifters should do community service by . . .

C   Make a list of details or examples to support your thesis statement.

D   Use your thesis statement and the supporting examples to write a composition with an introductory paragraph containing your opinion, and at least one paragraph with supporting examples or details.

E   **Pair work**   Take turns reading each other's compositions. Can you think of additional examples or details your partner could use to be more persuasive?

Lesson **B** *Consumer beware*

Shopping options

starting point

A **Pair work** Look at these three different ways you can buy things. What are the advantages of each type of shopping? Choose ideas from the list, and add others of your own.

shopping at a street market

shopping on-line

shopping from a catalog

▶ It isn't necessary for you to leave your home.
▶ You can get things at bargain prices.
▶ You can insist that they show you the actual product before you buy it.
▶ You can see the latest products before they reach the stores.
▶ You can request that the seller give you a lower price.
▶ _____
▶ _____

B **Pair work** What are the best ways to shop for these items? Discuss your answers.

an antique chair   a camera   clothes   a computer   fresh fruit   jewelry

A: I always buy my clothes at a department store. I would never buy clothes from a mail-order catalog or at a street market.
B: Why not?
A: I think it's important to try on clothes before you buy them.

Shopping preferences

listening

 Listen to Ken and Anna talk about their shopping preferences, and complete the chart.

	Where they shop	Reason
Ken		
Anna		

3 Verbs in the subjunctive

grammar focus

Certain verbs and expressions are followed by the subjunctive. The subjunctive uses the simple or base form of the verb.

These verbs are almost always followed by the subjunctive.

demand   insist   propose   recommend   request   suggest

Jim's brother suggested (that) **he stop** spending so much money.
His daughter proposed (that) **he keep** a list of weekly expenses.
Jim's wife recommended (that) **he talk** with a financial counselor.

These expressions are frequently followed by the subjunctive, but they can also be followed by an infinitive.

it is crucial   it is imperative   it is necessary
it is essential   it is important   it is vital

It is necessary that **couples discuss** financial problems openly.
It is necessary for **couples to discuss** financial problems openly.

A Use verbs followed by the subjunctive instead of *should* or *must* to complete these sentences without changing the meaning. Then compare your answers with a partner.

1. Our family should try to cut down on expenses.
   I suggested that . . .

   I suggested that our family try to cut down on expenses.

2. We should limit how much money we spend.
   It is essential that . . .
3. Everyone in the family must cooperate.
   It is crucial that . . .
4. Each person in the family should have a budget.
   My son suggested that . . .
5. We should shop at bargain stores.
   My daughter proposed that . . .
6. She should buy only clothes that she will wear often.
   I said it was imperative that . . .

B Group work Use these verbs and expressions to give the people below some advice on how to overcome their shopping problems. Have you ever had a similar problem? Ask your group for advice.

advise   propose   recommend   suggest   it is crucial   it is essential

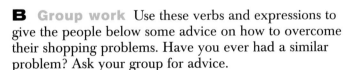

"Many times I buy shoes that fit me well in the store, but when I wear them later at home, they're too tight. I feel as though my feet shrink when I'm in the store!"

"When I go shopping, I set a limit on how much money I'll spend, but I always end up going at least fifty percent above my original budget."

"My credit cards have been canceled twice over the last few months because I always forget to pay my bills on time. I feel really embarrassed when that happens, but I can't help it!"

Marketing strategies

vocabulary   **A** Pair work Look at the expressions below used to describe types of advertising. Discuss any unfamiliar terms with your partner. What can each type of advertising be used to promote?

airplane banners	full-page ads
billboards	Internet banners
blimps	radio commercials
classified ads	telemarketing
flyers	TV commercials
free samples	

B Group work Have you bought anything recently as a result of advertising? What was it? Were you satisfied with what you bought?

> *Well, I got a call from a telemarketer recently. She offered me two free theater tickets if I subscribed to a new magazine. It seemed like a good deal.*

The power of advertising

discussion   **A** Group work Discuss these questions and give reasons for your answers. Then compare your opinions with those of your classmates.

> ▶ Which type of advertising above is the most effective?
> ▶ Which type of advertising influences you the most?
> ▶ What's the most original advertisement or TV commercial you've seen recently?
> ▶ Are there any advertisements you've seen recently that bothered you in some way? What didn't you like about them?

> *I think TV commercials are the most effective. Everyone watches TV.*

> *Yes, and even if you don't pay attention to commercials, they still affect you.*

B Pair work Some people think there should be more laws to regulate advertising. Write down three laws you think are especially important and should be passed if they do not already exist. Share your opinions with the class.

> *Commercials that advertise cigarettes should not be allowed on television.*

reading **A** **Pair work** Brainstorm a list of things you think people should be careful about when buying merchandise on the Internet. Then read the article, and compare your ideas with the writer's.

Buying from Home

Each year people around the world spend billions of dollars buying merchandise on the Internet. Here are some tips on how to save money and protect yourself when shopping on-line.

▶ **Shop around.** Try several Web sites to be sure you are getting the lowest price possible. *Consumer Reports* asked 30 people to shop on-line for the same items with these results: the price of a white polo shirt ranged from $12 to $35.99; a certain computer game cost from $18.95 to $34.95.

▶ **Check shipping and handling charges.** Your bargain purchase may turn out not to be a bargain after you add in the shipping and handling charges. Sometimes you don't find out the total you will have to pay until you have submitted your on-line purchase form and the total is confirmed. Some programs automatically charge you an expensive overnight or two-day delivery fee unless you are careful to change it to a less costly alternative.

▶ **Stick with companies you know.** Buy from companies that you trust. Don't buy from a Web site unless they list a toll-free number so that you can call their customer service department if there is a problem.

▶ **Use your credit card.** Most credit card companies offer some protection against poor quality merchandise or damaged goods. It's a good idea to download and print out a copy of the ordering information for your records.

▶ **Look for security guarantees.** If you have to give your credit card number, be sure that the program switches you to a secure screen to do this. Look for a picture of a key or a picture of a closed lock on the screen.

Source: Consumer Reports Online

B **Group work** Discuss these questions. Then share your answers with the class.

1. Have you ever bought anything on the Internet? What motivated you to do so?
2. How many people do you know who shop on-line? How do they feel about it?
3. How much time are you willing to spend on-line looking for the best price for an item? Is it worthwhile spending this much time?
4. Do you think it's safe to give your credit card number to a company on-line? Why or why not?

1 Animal quiz

starting point

A Can you match these animals with the comments below? Check your answers on p. 118.

dog **frog** **goose** **whale**

1. Whoever hunts one of these animals could be contributing to its extinction because it is an endangered species. ___whale___

2. This tiny creature seems to be giving us a serious ecological warning, and whatever is killing it is probably a serious environmental danger to all life on earth. _____

3. This animal is used in airports because it can smell whatever passengers try to hide in their luggage – food, drugs, etc. _____

4. This animal mates for life and will bond permanently with whoever spends time with it when it is young. _____

B Group work Can you think of three interesting facts about animals? Share them in groups, and answer any questions.

A: Did you know that some parrots can live to be over 80 years old?
B: Really? What kinds of parrots?

2 Animal kingdom

vocabulary

A Match these categories with their definitions. Then check your answers on p. 118.

1. amphibian _b_	a.	the order to which humans, apes, and monkeys belong
2. mammal ____	b.	an animal that lives both on land and in water
3. primate ____	c.	an animal whose blood temperature changes with the outside temperature and whose body is covered by scales or plates
4. reptile ____	d.	an animal in which the female gives birth to babies, not eggs, and feeds them on milk from her own body
5. rodent ____	e.	a type of small mammal with sharp front teeth

B Pair work Think of an animal for each category, and compare your answers.

Noun clauses with whoever and whatever

grammar
focus

Whoever and *whatever* can begin noun clauses. They can function as either the subject or object of the clause.

whoever = the person who/anyone who/everyone who
Whoever hunts endangered species could be contributing to their extinction.
Some animals will bond permanently with **whoever** spends time with them when they are young.

whatever = anything that/everything that
The international community should do **whatever** is necessary to protect endangered species.
Trained dogs can smell **whatever** passengers try to hide in their luggage.

A Complete the sentences with *whoever* or *whatever*. Then compare your answers with a partner.

1. ___Whoever___ feeds wild animals is doing them a disservice because this can alter their feeding and migration patterns.
2. _____ sees a poisonous snake should try not to make any sudden moves because snakes are attracted to _____ they see moving near them.
3. A cobra will strike _____ crosses its path, and it is so poisonous that a tablespoon of its venom can kill 165 people.
4. Rodents will chew on _____ they find in their environment.
5. _____ encounters a racoon should stay away from it because it will attack humans if it feels cornered.
6. People usually think of giraffes as beautiful, peaceful creatures, but a giraffe can quickly become aggressive with _____ comes too close to it.

B Group work Complete the following statements about animals with your own point of view. Compare and discuss your ideas with the other members of your group.

1. Governments should do whatever is necessary to create more wild animal preserves, including . . .

Governments should do whatever is necessary to create more wild animal preserves, including raising money through environmental awareness campaigns.

2. Whoever thinks that rodents and reptiles are repulsive animals . . .
3. Whatever is causing the disappearance of frogs and other amphibians . . .
4. Whoever wears a fur coat . . .
5. Animals are part of our natural environment. Whatever . . .

A: I think governments should do whatever is necessary to create more wild animal preserves. They should raise money through environmental awareness campaigns.
B: Maybe people could make voluntary contributions when they file their taxes.
C: That's a good idea. That way whoever wants to contribute can, but it's not obligatory.

Lesson A A wild bunch! 75

discussion **Group work** Read these facts about endangered species, and discuss the questions below with your group.

Did you know that . . . ?

✶ Once found throughout Africa and Asia, cheetahs are now only scattered through eastern Africa and through a region of southwestern Africa.

✶ There are only about 20 Siberian tigers left in the wild in China. Around 100 live in Chinese zoos and animal parks.

✶ It is estimated that only 1,000 pandas remain in the wild.

✶ Some experts estimate that tigers die at the rate of one a day. There are only about 5,000 left.

✶ Mountain gorillas and humans have about 97 percent of their DNA in common. For this reason, many human illnesses are transmitted to these animals, contributing to their gradual extinction.

1. Can you think of some reasons why species become endangered?
2. Do you think it's important to protect them?
3. What animals in your country are in danger of disappearing?
4. Are there any laws in your country to protect endangered species?

5 **Save the animals.**

listening **A** Listen to these reports about endangered species. As you hear each description, write the name of the animal.

panda

snow leopard

orangutan

Animal 1 _____ **Animal 2** _____ **Animal 3** _____

B **Pair work** How could we save the animals mentioned in Exercise A? Write three laws to protect these animals.

C **Class activity** Present the laws that you wrote. Answer questions from your classmates.

writing

In persuasive writing, you take a position on an issue and try to convince the reader that your position is correct. To do so, you should provide examples and reasons that support your case. You should also present the opposing point of view and argue against it.

A Read the following composition. What is the writer's position? What are the reasons the writer gives to support the position? Is the writer's case convincing?

A Law to Help Protect Endangered Species

Many species are now in danger of becoming extinct. Among the threats to endangered species are businesses that buy and sell animals for their skin and other parts. Unfortunately, the people who run these businesses are not discouraged by fines, which they see as just another business expense. A better way to control the problem would be to force whoever is caught buying or selling products made from endangered species to do community service. Their community service should require work that helps protect the animals they are harming.

Such a law could be quite effective. If people trafficking in illegal animal products were forced to help endangered species, they might understand how destructive their business is. Also, their community service tasks would turn them into helpers rather than destroyers. . . .

Some might say that community service would not be an effective way to protect endangered species because it would not really convince people to abandon a profitable business. However, community service would be much more effective than fines alone. Paying a fine is as easy as writing a check, but doing community service means . . .

We must do whatever we can to save all species so that the complex web of life is protected. For this reason, we need stronger, more effective penalties such as the one I am proposing.

B Pair work With a partner, take a position on an issue related to animals or endangered species. Then brainstorm reasons supporting this position.

C Write a multi-paragraph composition supporting your position with the reasons you have brainstormed. Make sure you argue against the opposing position.

D Pair work Take turns reading your compositions. Your partner will suggest ways your writing could be made more persuasive.

"Man's best friend"

 Pet demographics in the U.S.

starting point Read this information about pet ownership in the United States, and discuss the questions below.

59% of U.S. households have at least one pet.

28% of U.S. homes have at least one dog.

21% of households in the U.S. have at least one cat.

53% of married couples with children have pets.

1.5% of U.S. households have reptiles as pets.

The number of households with a dog has declined 18% in the last 20 years.

Bird ownership has soared 15% in the past 5 years.

1. Why do you think dogs and cats make good pets?
2. What are two advantages and disadvantages of having a pet?
3. What do you think people find interesting about having reptiles as pets? Would you like to have one?
4. What kinds of pets do you prefer?
5. Have you ever had a pet? If so, what kind?

 Common ideas about pets

discussion **Pair work** Read these statements about pets. Do you agree with them? Discuss your point of view with your partner.

	Agree	Not Sure	Disagree
1. It's a mistake to keep unusual pets, such as a snake or a rat. Whenever someone has an unusual pet, it's sure to cause problems.	☐	☐	☐
2. Dogs and cats can't live in the same house. They fight whenever they are together.	☐	☐	☐
3. Taking a dog for a walk is a good way to relax whenever you feel tense.	☐	☐	☐
4. Cats are cute when they're kittens, but they're unpleasant when they're older.	☐	☐	☐
5. Wherever there are pets, there is an increased risk of disease.	☐	☐	☐

I would never have a snake or a rat. What if a child let it out of its cage and it escaped?

Yes, but I don't have kids, and I think snakes are interesting. Everyone has a cat or a dog, and I like pets that are different.

3 Whenever *and* wherever *contrasted with* when *and* where

Whenever and *wherever* introduce adverbial clauses. Notice their position in the sentence.

Whenever I go away on a trip, my dog becomes very lonely.
My dog becomes very lonely **whenever I go away on a trip.**
Wherever I go, my cat follows me.
My cat follows me **wherever I go.**

Note that *whenever* and *wherever* mean "at any time" and "in any place." Sometimes *when* and *where* can be used interchangeably with *whenever* and *wherever*.

Whenever I go away, my dog misses me.
When I go away, my dog misses me.

Whenever and *wherever* cannot be used if the sentence refers to a specific time or location.

My dog would jump up and lick me **whenever** I came home after a long trip. (at any time)
My dog knocked over a vase **when** he jumped over the living room table. (specific time)
Once we let the bird out of its cage so it could fly **wherever** it wanted. (any place)
The cat is sleeping under the chair **where** it feels safe from visitors. (specific place)

A Complete the sentences using *whenever* or *wherever*. If the time or place is specific, use *when* or *where*. More than one answer may be possible.

1. Dogs are good traveling companions. They will go ____wherever____ you take them.
2. People with respiratory allergies will sneeze _____ they are near a cat or a dog.
3. It is not true that dogs wag their tail _____ they are happy. Sometimes they do it precisely _____ they're nervous or about to attack.
4. Large dogs should be taken almost daily to a place _____ they can run and exercise for at least one hour.
5. Female dogs can be completely trained to hunt _____ they're a year old. With most males, however, trainers need to wait until the dog is two years old.

B **Pair work** Complete the chart below with your opinions. Then write four sentences about pets using *whenever, wherever, when,* or *where*. Discuss your answers with a partner.

Type of pet	Best place to keep it	Best time to get it	Places for it to go	Times to feed it
A dog		when you are young	wherever it wants	
A cat	anywhere at home			morning, evening
A bird				
A snake				

A: The best time to get a dog is when you're young.
B: I agree. Children have more time to spend with animals.

4

People and animals

discussion **Pair work** People interact with animals in many ways. Look at these pictures, and discuss the questions below.

1. Which of the activities above do you find acceptable? Which do you feel are not?
2. What are some other animals that people commonly interact with in these places?
3. What are some other purposes for which animals are used?

> I don't see anything wrong with keeping animals as pets as long as they are well taken care of.

> I'm not sure I agree. For one thing, they can disturb the neighbors. In my building, pets aren't allowed.

5 **Working animals**

listening   Listen to some of the types of work that animals can do to help people, and complete the chart. Which of them do you consider the most surprising?

Animal	How it helps people

6 **Is it right to do that?**

discussion Read these statements about animals. Then discuss the issues with your classmates. Do you agree?

1. Using animals for medical research is unpleasant but necessary.
2. We should all be vegetarians. Eating meat is unhealthy, immoral, and not ecological.
3. Governments should ban hunting.
4. Killing animals for their fur is unethical and unnecessary.
5. It is inhumane to use animals for cosmetics research.

reading **A** **Pair work** Discuss these questions. Then read the article.

1. Have you heard any stories about using animals in search-and-rescue missions? What are they?
2. Which animal do you think is most useful for rescue missions? Why?

Shirley and Cinnamon

In September 1985, an earthquake devastated Mexico City and claimed more than 6,000 lives. But the rescuers had help in saving the survivors who were trapped under several floors of steel and concrete. Shirley Hammond and her search dog named Cinnamon were among the 13 teams of dogs and handlers from the United States that assisted in the search through the rubble of the central district of Mexico City.

Shirley and Cinnamon slowly made their way to the area where some workers thought they had heard voices. Shirley knew from her training that Cinnamon would stay focused while crawling toward an area of concrete rubble. The dog began sniffing and pawing at the rubble. Then she barked and pawed more intensely. She had detected human scent. Shirley knew she had to call for another dog to confirm the alert before they could commit resources to a long and grueling rescue effort. But in a short time, another team arrived and confirmed Cinnamon's findings. It took several days to reach the 12 trapped factory workers.

"Nothing is more exciting than finding someone who is trapped or lost," says Shirley. She says that the ability of the dogs to find people never ceases to amaze her. She notes that during rescue missions the dogs are supposed to alert their handlers only to live people, as opposed to those who have died, or to live animals. "How dogs tell when someone is alive, I really have no idea," says Shirley. "But I am certainly happy that they can."

Both dogs and handlers must go through an extensive training program to be certified rescuers. The handler requires much more training than the dog because the trainer must learn to understand the meaning of what the dog is communicating. The dogs are trained to find humans in a specific area by recognizing a human scent and footprints. It can take three or four years to get a dog certified, and it can cost about $15,000. The training is arduous, but the people and dogs who make it through are skilled in a wide variety of ways. They are the ones you would want looking for you if you were trapped or lost.

Source: "That Others May Live: Canine Search and Rescue," www.Petsource.com

B **Group work** Discuss these questions.

1. What are the advantages of using dogs in rescue missions?
2. Do you feel it is acceptable to subject dogs to danger?

1 Relative pronouns in defining relative clauses

A Complete these sentences with *who, whom, that, which, whose,* or no pronoun.

1. More and more people are rejecting foods ___*that*___ do not come from local producers.
2. Working from home via the Internet is a possibility _____ many people are exploring.
3. Many people _____ moved to the country are now returning to the city.
4. Young people are returning to traditional beliefs _____ their parents rejected.
5. Parents _____ children are in college are working longer hours to pay their tuition.
6. Natural remedies are something _____ more people are experimenting with these days.

B Write five sentences about changes taking place in your country or community. Use at least four of the relative pronouns in Exercise A. Then discuss with a partner.

A lot of people who never used to pay attention to their diet are eating healthier food.

2 As if, as though, as, the way, *and* like

A Complete these sentences with *as if, as though, as, the way,* or *like.* More than one answer may be possible.

1. I don't have as many unrealistic goals ___*as*___ I did when I was younger.
2. Sometimes I still think _____ I did when I was a child.
3. I feel _____ I'm always forgetting to do something, and that puts a lot of stress on me.
4. I have so many daily routines that sometimes I feel _____ I'm an automated robot.
5. I wish I could still believe all things were possible, _____ I did some years ago.

B **Pair work** Discuss the statements in Exercise A with a partner. Which are true for you?

3 Placement of direct and indirect objects

A Complete these sentences using the words in parentheses. If more than one answer is possible, write the sentence two ways.

1. My car is almost ten years old, but it cost . . . at the time. (a fortune/me)

   My car is almost ten years old, but it cost me a fortune at the time.

2. The salespeople recommended . . . , and so I chose a car that had them. (antilock brakes/me)
3. They explained . . . as well. (the benefits of dual air bags/me)
4. It still runs, but now I'm thinking of giving . . . (my car/my sister)
5. I mentioned . . . , and she was thrilled. (the idea/her)

B **Pair work** Describe something you own that you would like to give away. Explain why.

4 Verbs in the subjunctive

A Read this excerpt from a travel guide about shopping in Chiang Mai, Thailand. Then rewrite the article completing it with appropriate verbs and expressions from the list below.

propose   recommend   suggest   it is important   it is necessary

When shopping at the night market in Chiang Mai, we _____ that travelers allow themselves plenty of time. We _____ that bargain hunters spend no less than a full evening to take in the entire market. We _____ that they see as much of what's available before making any major purchases. There is so much to buy! _____ that travelers budget their money carefully.

B Pair work Take turns asking each other about shopping in your city. Use verbs in the subjunctive to answer these questions.

1. Where can I find the best deals on clothes?
2. What stores do you suggest for locally made items?
3. What store do you recommend for CDs and videos?
4. Are there any stores that are especially worth visiting?
5. What general advice do you have about finding the best bargains here?

> I would recommend that you go to . . .

5 Noun clauses with whoever and whatever

Rewrite these sentences by replacing the subject or object of the appropriate clause with *whoever* or *whatever*.

1. Anyone who has wild animals at home should be careful because many of them will not recognize their owners when they grow up.

   Whoever has wild animals at home should be careful . . .

2. Cobras simply follow anything that moves in front of them.
3. Environmentalists these days are doing anything that is legal in order to protect some species from poachers. They are even painting the animal's fur so it cannot be used to make coats.
4. Villagers in some parts of Africa fear stampedes because the frightened animals can destroy anything that gets in their way.
5. In many countries, anyone who kills an endangered animal could receive a serious fine.

6 Whenever and wherever contrasted with when and where

Pair work Complete these sentences with *whenever, wherever, when,* or *where.* Compare your answers with a partner, and explain the reasons for your choices. More than one answer may be possible.

1. _____ there are furry animals, there is a potential health hazard because they carry dust in their hair. That's why dogs and cats are not appropriate pets.
2. Cities should have more places _____ people can take their dogs because it is very annoying to be around dogs in parks and other public areas.
3. Dogs are very affectionate animals, especially _____ they sense that their owner is not feeling well.
4. Some people abandon their pets _____ they travel. That is cruel because the animals would never abandon their owners.

A Read what these people have to say about recent trends. Who do you agree with the most, and who do you agree with the least? Give reasons to support your ideas.

Debbie

"I think it's appalling the way people risk their health by experimenting with alternative medicines and therapies. No one can be sure of the safety of these things. This is one trend I find upsetting."

Ralph

"It's intriguing that many younger people are now returning to the values we rejected in our youth. I never thought I'd see my own son getting married at such a young age and attending religious services. It's remarkable."

Stephanie

"I feel it's absurd the way some people spend all their time and money on health and fitness in order to look like they've just stepped out of a fashion magazine. There are more important things in life than looking good. It's just absurd."

> I don't think alternative medicine is dangerous. You just have to be careful and use common sense in making decisions.

B Group work Discuss how you feel about these life choices and other life choices you know about. Then share your answers with the class.

▶ adult children returning home to live with their parents

▶ people choosing to adopt children rather than have children of their own

▶ senior citizens going back to school to earn degrees

▶ people forming friendships and support groups on the Internet

▶ people choosing to spend their free time doing volunteer work

8 | **Shopping advantages**

Pair work From which of these places would you be most likely and least likely to buy the things in the pictures? Share your ideas with the class.

a small grocery store   the Internet   a street market   a department store   a drugstore

9 **New products and marketing plans**

A Group work Think of a new product or service you think would be successful. What is it? How does it work? What's the best way to advertise and promote it?

A: Well, what I'm thinking about is a concierge service for people who are new in town.
B: The concierge would provide the same services as a concierge in a hotel. We'd offer information and advice on . . . as well as . . .
C: Great! And we could make flyers to promote the service and put them . . .

B Present your product and advertising plan to the class. Who has the best product and the best ideas for promoting it?

10 **Suitable pets?**

Pair work Would you consider keeping any of these animals as pets? Why or why not?

boa constrictor

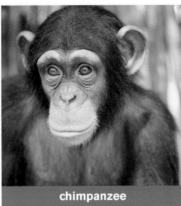
chimpanzee

lizard

Well, I might keep a chimpanzee as a pet because chimpanzees are very intelligent.

11 **Animal issues**

Group work Discuss these statements in groups. Which do you agree and disagree with? Give reasons to support your answers.

▸ Every animal on earth is important, and the extinction of one threatens us all.
▸ Hunting should be encouraged as it's an effective way to control animal populations.
▸ Zoos ought to be abolished since they do nothing to educate people about animals.
▸ People must realize that urban development is more important than animal habitats.
▸ Already many species of animals have become extinct, and it hasn't created any problem.
▸ Strong laws must be passed to protect the rights of animals.
▸ An animal has the same right to life as a person does.
▸ Medical science could not have progressed as far as it has without animal research.

A: I agree with the first statement. Animals are dependent on each other for food.
B: Yes, that's true. Killing them . . .

Lesson A *The nature of language*

1 Spoken and written language

starting point

A Read these texts. Which of the topics is each one about? Which do you think are spoken language? written language?

management skills   increase in productivity   new product

1. That's impossible! I'm working at top speed already, and I got lucky on a few big orders in the first quarter. That's why I'm 20% ahead of my quota right now. . . .
increase in productivity
spoken language

2. The photocopy machines in the catalog you showed me seem to be greatly superior to the ones we're currently using. Most of our machines need to be replaced. . . .

3. Increasing productivity is going to be a challenge. A combination of circumstances has helped to make my 20% gain possible so far. I don't believe the 25% is realistic. . . .

4. Well, neither Julia nor Joe was able to improve morale. The department was sort of a mess before I took over. . . .

5. This is state of the art! Why don't we show it to Tom? Maybe he'll get rid of those dinosaurs we have in the copy room. None of them works well. . . .

6. During my tenure as department manager, morale improved significantly. Now each of the workers has an annual performance review. . . .

B **Pair work** Can you think of some features of spoken and written language? Share your ideas with the class.

> In spoken language, more idioms are used, and the vocabulary chosen is more informal.

2 What's correct language?

discussion

Read the following comments about the use of language, and complete the chart. Discuss your opinions with a partner.

	Agree	Disagree
1. Most people don't speak their first language correctly.	☐	☐
2. Learning grammar doesn't help a person speak a language any better.	☐	☐
3. E-mail is causing people to write more carelessly.	☐	☐
4. Teaching writing is unnecessary. People learn as they go along.	☐	☐
5. Young people nowadays don't pay any attention to correct language.	☐	☐

> I don't agree with the first one. Of course people speak their first language correctly. After all, who could speak it "better" than a native speaker?

grammar focus

Subject-verb agreement in sentences with quantifiers

Some collective nouns, such as *staff, majority,* and *minority,* can have a singular or plural verb. If the noun refers to the individual members of a unit, the verb is plural.

The **majority** *of people* in the world **speak** more than one language.
Only a **minority** *of U.S. students* **write** correctly when they enter college.

If the noun refers to a whole unit, the verb is singular.

In the U.S., **Spanish speakers** constitute a linguistic **minority** that **is** growing rapidly.

None, each, and *every one* are followed by a singular verb.

None of my friends **knows** how to write good business letters.
Each of the instructors in the school **has** a different teaching style.

All (of), a lot of, lots of, some, most, plenty, and fractions are followed by a singular verb if the noun they modify is uncountable or singular and by a plural verb if the noun they modify is plural.

A lot of *contact* with native speakers **helps** to learn a second language better.
Half of *the textbook* **is** about improving your communication skills.
A lot of *second language learners* **have** difficulty using informal English.
Half of *the chapters* in the book **deal** with improving writing skills.

A Complete these sentences with the correct form of the verb in parentheses.

1. A lot of people ___*feel*___ that slang is inappropriate in writing. (feel)
2. The staff at school _____ able to speak at least three languages. (be)
3. All of the employees in my company _____ to take a business communication course. (have)
4. A lot of the language that people use every day _____ inappropriate in writing. (be)
5. Every one of the letters I receive usually _____ one or two spelling mistakes. (contain)
6. None of my friends _____ foreign newspapers regularly. (read)
7. A lot of college students really _____ from taking debate courses early on in their studies. (benefit)
8. Some of my friends _____ thinking about taking a pronunciation course next semester. (be)

B **Group work** Complete these sentences with information about how people use language in different situations. Then discuss your answers.

1. Most of the announcers you hear on the radio . . .
2. The majority of people my age . . .
3. A lot of the language young people use . . .
4. None of my friends . . .
5. A lot of the slang expressions people use these days . . .
6. Nowadays some of the language you hear in movies . . .

A: Most of the announcers you hear on the radio have a very formal way of speaking. They don't speak the way ordinary people do.
B: Maybe, but I think that's changing. For example, . . .

4 Idiomatic expressions

vocabulary **A** The expressions below can be used to comment on people and the way they speak. Do you know what they mean? Which ones are positive, and which ones are negative?

Jack is sort of a windbag.
Mei-Li has a way with words.
Alex can never stick to the point.
Jennifer loves to hear herself talk.
With Carlos, you can't get a word
 in edgewise.
Somsak never talks behind your back.
Kate can talk you into anything.
Steve has a very sharp tongue.

B **Group work** Have you ever known anyone you would describe with one of the expressions above? Tell your group.

> My neighbor John is sort of a windbag. He talks too much, and he's always trying to show how important he is.

5 Practical advice

discussion **A** **Pair work** People often tell stories about what has happened to them or to other people. Read this advice from a conversation manual. Do you agree with it? What other advice would you give?

- Don't tell a story that is too long.
- Don't give unnecessary details.
- Don't be the first to laugh at your own story.
- Don't start a story unless you're sure how it ends.

B **Group work** Think of a story to share with your classmates. Describe something interesting that has happened to you or that you have heard about recently. Try to follow the guidelines in Exercise A.

A: The other day I nearly got into an accident.
B: What happened?
A: Well, I was driving on Route 60 when this guy in front of me . . .

6 Storytellers

listening   Listen to these people's anecdotes. Decide if each anecdote is interesting or not. Give reasons.

Is it interesting?	Why or why not?

writing

When you write a summary, state in your own words the main ideas of a text, leaving out most of the supporting details. The summary must accurately reflect the ideas of the original text.

A Read the passage and then the summary below it. Match the main ideas in the summary with the parts of the original passage that express those ideas. What has been left out of the summary?

CONVERSATIONAL TURNS

Probably the most widely recognized conversational convention is that people take turns speaking. But how do people know when it is their turn? Some rules must be present, otherwise conversations would be continually breaking down into a disorganized jumble of interruptions and simultaneous talk.

Turn-taking cues are usually quite subtle. People do not simply stop talking when they are ready to yield the floor. They usually signal in advance that they are about to conclude. The clues may be semantic ("So anyway, . . ." or "Last but not least, . . ."); but more commonly the speech itself can be modified to show that a turn is about to end – typically, by lowering its pitch, loudness, or speed.

Body movements and patterns of eye contact are especially important. While speaking, we look at and away from our listener in about equal proportions; but as we approach the end of a turn, we look at the listener more steadily.

Listeners are not passive in all of this. Here too there are several ways of signaling that someone wants to speak next. One way is through an observable increase in body tension – by leaning forward or producing an audible intake of breath. A less subtle approach is simply to interrupt – a strategy that may be tolerated, if the purpose is to clarify what the speaker is saying, but that more usually leads to social disapproval.

Source: *The Cambridge Encyclopedia of Language* by David Crystal

Summary

Turn-taking is a way of organizing conversation so that people don't interrupt each other or talk at the same time. Some ways of signaling when you are about to stop talking are using specific phrases; changing pitch, loudness, or speed; and looking more steadily at the listener. Listeners may show they want to talk by tensing up, leaning forward, or simply interrupting, which people disapprove of unless it's done for clarification.

B Pair work Turn to the reading in Lesson B, or choose your own article on language or a related topic. Follow these steps.

1. With your partner, choose an important paragraph.
2. Separately, write one sentence that gives the main idea of that paragraph.
3. Now compare your work with that of your partner. Which sentence expresses the main idea better?

C Write a summary of all or part of the whole article in one or more paragraphs.

D Pair work Compare your summary with your partner's, and critique each other's work. Which one expresses the main ideas of the article more accurately?

1 Are you afraid to talk?

starting point

A Are you uncomfortable speaking in front of others? Complete the chart. Then add one more statement of your own.

	always true	sometimes true	never true
1. I can't sleep the night before a presentation.	☐	☐	☐
2. I rarely participate in discussions at work or in class.	☐	☐	☐
3. I avoid situations in which I might have to give an impromptu speech.	☐	☐	☐
4. When talking to others, I find it hard to look people in the eye.	☐	☐	☐
5. I can speak only from a prepared speech.	☐	☐	☐
6. I am intimidated by job interviews.	☐	☐	☐
7. I'd rather go to the dentist, pay taxes, or clean closets than give a presentation.	☐	☐	☐
8. _____	☐	☐	☐

Source: *Schaum's Quick Guide to Great Presentation Skills*

B **Pair work** Compare your answers with those of a partner. How are you different?

C **Group work** Join another pair. Make a list of practical suggestions for being a public speaker. Share your suggestions with the class.

> **Words of advice**
>
> One thing to remember is . . .
> It's important to . . .
> You need to try to . . .

2 Making a good impression

discussion

Pair work Read about these people's experiences. What could they have done to overcome their problems? Discuss each problem with a partner.

Diane

"I'm sure I could have been offered a very good job, but I got nervous in the interview and talked too much."

Young-joon

"I could have been hired by an international company, but I need to speak English better. My vocabulary isn't large enough."

Carmen

"I've been told by friends that I come across as cold and unfriendly over the phone, although I'm not really like that."

> *Diane should have listened more and just answered the questions they asked her.*

> *I agree. She should also have prepared an outline of what she was going to say.*

grammar focus

Overview of passives

Passive sentences put emphasis on the person or thing affected by the action. The agent may be omitted when it is not relevant.

passive = subject + a form of be + past participle

Notice these examples in different tenses.

Simple present: Composition **is** more frequently **taught** in advanced classes.

Present continuous: These days high school students **are being asked** to read more than ever before.

Simple past: In the past, students **were** frequently **asked** to memorize grammar rules out of context.

Past continuous: Sometimes students didn't know how to use the grammar structures they **were being taught**.

Present perfect: I **have been told** that I speak too quickly.

Future with *going to*: In a few years from now, multimedia materials **are going to be used** in every language classroom.

Modals: Students **should be** constantly **encouraged** to participate in class discussions.

Past modals: My friend Diane **could have been offered** a very good job, but she got very nervous in the interview.

A Complete these sentences with information about language that is true for you or that reflects your opinion. Then add two more sentences of your own using some of the passive verb forms from the grammar box.

1. I've been told by many people that . . .

   I've been told by many people that my English sounds too formal.

2. My classmates and I are constantly encouraged to . . .
3. I hope that someday I will be offered . . .
4. I felt I was being pushed too hard when we were studying . . .
5. Not long ago I was told that . . .
6. In my opinion, languages should be taught . . .
7. I've been advised . . .
8. University students should/shouldn't be forced to . . .
9. _____
10. _____

The friend with whom I traveled was very congenial.

B **Pair work** Compare your answers to Exercise A with a partner. Ask and answer follow-up questions.

A: I've been told by many people that my English sounds too formal.
B: Really? Who told you that?
A: Usually native speakers tell me that I sound like a book. I guess that's because . . .

discussion   **Pair work** Read these ads announcing workshops for improving communication skills. When would each set of skills be useful in everyday life? Would you be interested in any of the workshops? Why?

HOW TO TALK WITH ANYONE	**VERBAL SELF-DEFENSE**	**PRESENTATION SKILLS**
Never fear small talk again! Find out how you can develop the charisma to take you to the next level in the business world or to attract your perfect mate. Learn to:	Do you often find yourself saying something, only to wish you could take it back? In this workshop, we'll give you solid techniques and strategies to:	Do you panic every time you have to give a presentation? It's time to learn skills for developing a natural and convincing style so you can give memorable presentations. In this seminar, you will learn how to:
• **Develop a dynamic personality** • **Use communication skills for business, personal life, and pleasure** • **Naturally attract other charismatic people**	• **Detect, disarm, and defuse any verbal conflict** • **Control your emotions so they don't control you** • **Stand up for yourself without stepping on someone's toes**	• **Calm your nerves to help concentrate on your presentation** • **Command attention and respect from your audience** • **Use your speech to create a presence and enhance your image**

A: I think I could benefit from the "Verbal Self-Defense" seminar. Sometimes I have a problem controlling myself, and I say things that are completely out of line.
B: Maybe you don't really need to attend a seminar for that. You could work on it yourself.

listening   **A** Listen to a talk about speaking in public. Take notes on how to prepare and deliver a good presentation.

B **Pair work** Choose a topic that would be suitable for a four-minute class presentation. With your partner, brainstorm the information you will include and the order in which you will present it. Do not write your presentation in full.

C **Group work** Take turns giving your presentation in groups. Others will comment on the effectiveness of your presentation.

Presentation starters

I would like to tell you about...
This morning I would like to discuss...
The subject of my presentation is...

reading **A** Discuss these questions with a partner before reading the following article.

1. How would you define slang?
2. What slang words in English do you know? Where did you learn them?
3. Do you use slang when you speak English or your first language?
   Why or why not?

THE LONG HISTORY OF Slang

Slang that is still used today sometimes goes back as far as our oldest literature. Geoffrey Chaucer used "gab" for "talk," and William Shakespeare originally coined the phrase of agreement, "Right on!"

But most slang words and expressions come and go. Current popular slang includes "be a couch potato," "veg out," or "zone out." All express pretty much the same condition: to feel tired and not want to do anything other than sit on a couch. "To chill out" means to relax, even to become a lazy couch potato for a while.

Slang is often casual and used between friends. To criticize someone, people often resort to using slang. He was a "cheapskate," a "dimwit," a "flake," a "space cadet," a "worrywart"!

Slang also helps us to shock, to exaggerate. When you watch your baby learn to walk, it's not simply natural or cute, but "mind-blowing," or "phenomenal," and the baby is a "genius" and a "champ."

Slang is "hip." Slang is "cool." It represents a departure from what is traditional, and slang expressions can eventually become popular enough to replace the accepted ones. Slang allows us to break the ice and shift into a more casual and friendly gear. Maybe you, too, are a "hip" and "cool" person who prefers "What's happening?" to the more formal greeting, "How are you?"

B Group work Discuss these ideas. Then share your observations with the class.

1. Slang is just another word for "bad" English.
2. People use slang when they want to express their originality.
3. Slang is used among groups who share a common identity.

Lesson A   *Good science, bad science*

1 What's new?

starting point

A Read about these scientific breakthroughs. Which ones do you think offer benefits to humans? Which ones don't? Why?

DNA tracking

Scientists have discovered that every single person in the world has a unique gene pattern that can be detected in a single drop of blood.

antiaging discovery

Scientists have isolated the telomerase enzyme that prevents cells from aging. This discovery could significantly extend the human life span.

animal cloning

Scientists have been able to produce animal clones, exact genetic duplicates of the parent animal, since 1996.

B **Pair work** Read the information below about the discoveries in Exercise A, and indicate if each statement is a good idea (G) or a bad idea (B). Then discuss each statement with a partner.

1. The results of DNA testing have been used to help convict criminals. ____
2. All soldiers in the U.S. Army are required to give DNA samples. ____
3. Scientists want to begin testing the uses of telomerase on humans. ____
4. Telomerase research may make it possible for people to live for hundreds of years. ____
5. In 1998, President Clinton urged a ban on the cloning of human embryos. ____

2 The effects of technology

listening

A Listen to a reporter discussing genetically modified food. What are some advantages and disadvantages of this technology?

Advantages	Disadvantages

B **Pair work** Give an example of a new technology that has reshaped your daily life. What are the positive consequences? the negative consequences?

grammar focus

Indefinite and definite articles

Notice these rules for the indefinite articles *a* and *an* and the definite article *the*.

Countable nouns: Use an indefinite article (*a* or *an*) when you mention an item for the first time. When you refer to the same item again, use *the*.

They've just come out with **a computer** that doesn't need any wires. If **the computer** is not too far away from **a printer**, both machines can be connected through infrared rays.

If you use a plural noun to make a general statement, do not use an article. If you make the same statement using a singular noun, however, use *the*.

Computers are probably the greatest technological breakthrough of the last 100 years.
The computer is probably the greatest technological breakthrough of the last 100 years.

Uncountable nouns: Do not use an article with uncountable nouns (*technology, science, education, shopping, love,* etc.) when you are making a general statement. To refer to a specific type of technology, science, etc., *the* is generally used.

People rely too much on **technology** these days.
The technology used in today's computers is very different from **the technology** used in the first computers.

Superlative adjectives and sequence markers: Use *the* with superlatives and with the sequence markers *first, next, last,* etc., but not with time expressions such as *last night* or *next year*.

The lightest laptop computer currently available weighs less than a kilo.
The first computers were huge machines that were housed in large rooms.
The last time I bought a computer was two years ago.
Today's computers will become obsolete **next year**.

A Complete these sentences with the correct article. Put an X by sentences that do not need an article. Explain your answers to the class.

1. __X__ Internet shopping is becoming more and more popular.
2. _____ laptop computers are indispensable for people who work while they travel.
3. _____ computers used to fly airplanes make many of the decisions pilots used to make.
4. More and more products these days are incorporating _____ computers.
5. I hear they've invented _____ computer that can connect to the Internet without a phone wire.
6. _____ E-mail technology is affecting the way we live and think.
7. _____ last thing people should do is download Internet documents without knowing the source because that's how computer viruses are spread.
8. Not everyone believes that _____ technology has improved the quality of people's lives.

B **Pair work** Write statements about the things below. Add two more similar statements of your own. Then discuss your ideas with a partner.

1. the most interesting new product currently in stores
2. the biggest breakthrough in car technology
3. the most exciting new computer product on the market
4. the greatest advance in medicine
5. the most amazing invention of the twentieth century
6. _____
7. _____

> *The most interesting new product currently in stores is the flat screen TV. It looks very sleek and modern.*

> *Yes, I'd love to have one, except that they're so expensive.*

Good science, bad science

discussion **Group work** Look at these newspaper headlines. Discuss the positive and/or negative consequences of the events in the headlines.

Plastic Surgery Better and Cheaper Than Ever

SIXTY-YEAR-OLD GRANDMOTHER GIVES BIRTH

Pig Organs Save Human Lives

Microchip Implant Allows Criminals to Be Followed 24 Hours a Day

Prospective Parents Choose Child's Sex

A: I don't approve of so many people having plastic surgery.
B: But if it makes them feel more confident, isn't it a good thing?
C: Maybe. But I think it reinforces the idea that looks are what really counts.

5 **Scientific processes**

vocabulary **A** Match these words with their definitions. Check your answers on page 118.

1. conclusion _c_
2. consequence ___
3. discovery ___
4. invention ___
5. phenomenon ___
6. law ___
7. theory ___

a. the act of finding something that had not been known to exist before
b. a general rule that states what always happens when the same conditions exist
c. a judgment made after a lot of thought and consideration
d. something that happens, especially something unusual
e. a result of an action or a situation
f. something suggested as a reasonable explanation for evidence or facts
g. something newly designed or created

B Complete the sentences with words from Exercise A. Compare your answers with a partner.

1. The __discovery__ of DNA has helped police investigators solve otherwise impossible crime cases.
2. Isaac Newton supposedly worked out the _____ of gravity after watching an apple fall.
3. One _____ that currently exists about the origins of the universe is the concept of the Big Bang.
4. The _____ of the steam engine contributed significantly to the industrial revolution.
5. The tornado, also known as a twister, is a dangerous natural weather _____ that generates the world's highest-known wind speeds.
6. In the seventeenth century, Galileo reached the _____ that the sun did not revolve around the earth, but rather the earth revolved around the sun.
7. Scientists are still not sure what the _____ of consuming genetically modified food might be.

C **Pair work** Use three of the words in Exercise A to talk about scientific matters and discoveries.

> The loss of the ozone layer is a consequence of the production of too much carbon dioxide.

writing

A comparison/contrast essay presents the similarities and differences between two or more things. The thesis statement expresses your position on the subject, and the supporting paragraphs discuss similarities and differences.

A Read the essay. Then match each of the paragraphs to the headings below.

_____ introduction _____ differences between television and computers
_____ conclusion _____ similarities between television and computers

Television vs. computers

(1) Both television and computers have had an enormous impact on our lives, and although the influence of television seems to have reached its peak, the computer is proving to have profound and far-reaching effects on the way we do things.

(2) Television and computers provide quick access to information and entertainment; they are appealing to young audiences; and they both have something for everyone, day and night. Whether you want to check the weather, the stock market, or the latest music hit, either TV or a computer connected to the Internet is the medium of choice for many people. Television and computers are . . .

(3) Television has a great influence on the way that we think and talk and especially on the choices we make when we shop. However, as important as television is, it can be turned off and ignored. Computers, on the other hand, affect your life even if you don't use them at home or at work. Public transportation in large cities is likely to be controlled by a computer; your school records are probably somewhere in cyberspace; and maybe the shoes you're wearing were designed, not with pencil and paper, but on a computer screen. . . .

(4) Whereas television provides mainly information and entertainment, the computer already provides this and much more because of its many applications in all areas of business, industry, government, and our personal lives. In the near future, . . .

B Make a list of similarities and differences between two technological advances such as solar energy and nuclear energy, the telephone and E-mail, or any other pair you would like to write about.

C Write an essay comparing and contrasting the technological advances you chose. Make sure your essay has an introduction that includes a thesis statement, two paragraphs that describe similarities and differences, and a conclusion restating your point of view.

D **Pair work** Take turns reading your essays. Do not read your thesis statement. Can your partner guess your point of view?

1 It's simple!

starting point

A Look at these items, and read about how they work.

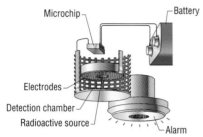

Microchip — Battery
Electrodes
Detection chamber
Radioactive source — Alarm

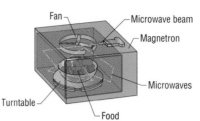

Fan — Microwave beam
Magnetron
Microwaves
Turntable
Food

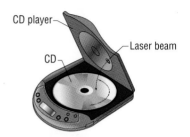

CD player
CD
Laser beam

smoke detector	microwave oven	compact disc
Many people have been using smoke detectors to protect their homes from fire since the 1970s. When a light beam in a smoke detector is interrupted by smoke in the air, a sensor reacts, triggering an alarm.	Microwave ovens have been a mainstay in American homes since their introduction into the market. A magnetron produces a beam of microwaves, which strike molecules of water in the food. Each wave of energy causes the molecules to move, producing heat.	Sales of compact discs (or CDs) have exceeded audiocassettes since the early 1990s, when people began to enjoy the many benefits of this new technology. Sound is digitally encoded on a disc. The disc is covered with a transparent coating so that the digital code can be read by a laser beam and then translated back into sound.

B Group work Can you explain how these common items work?

camera   hair dryer   lightbulb   toaster

> *A camera is a type of lightproof box with a shutter that opens briefly to allow in light. The light is projected through a lens onto a piece of film. . . .*

2 I can't cope with it!

listening

 Listen to a comedian talking about the difficulties he has coping with the technology in his house. List the items he mentions and what he finds particularly exasperating about each one.

Items	Problems

Present perfect and present perfect continuous tenses

The present perfect and present perfect continuous tenses can be used interchangeably to talk about an activity that continues into the present. They frequently occur with the expressions *since* and *for* and with the adverbs *lately* and *recently*.

Americans **have used** microwave ovens for a long time.
Americans **have been using** microwave ovens since the 1970s.
My parents **haven't used** their microwave lately.
My parents **haven't been using** their microwave recently.

The present perfect is used in many negative statements; with the adverbs *never, still, already*, and *yet*; and when stating the number of times an action has been repeated.

I **haven't used** my microwave oven for a long time.
I've **never cooked** any meat in my microwave oven.
Jim's microwave **has** already **had problems**, but he **hasn't done** anything about it yet.
I've **used** my microwave oven five times since I bought it.

Sometimes the present perfect focuses on the completion of an action, while the present perfect continuous emphasizes that an activity is still going on.

Elena **has installed** a smoke detector in her apartment. (completed action)
The landlord **has been installing** smoke detectors in all apartments. (activity still going on)

With stative (nonaction) verbs such as *like, be*, and *know*, the present perfect is generally used.
Scientists **have known** about genetic coding in DNA since the early 1950s.

A Complete these sentences with the present perfect or the present perfect continuous. More than one answer may be possible.

1. NASA _has built_ several successful space stations since the early 1970s. (build)
2. American astronauts _____ a total of more than 50,000 hours in space. (spend)
3. Records show that Russian pilots _____ this figure. (exceed)
4. Scientists _____ for many years that human bodies, like space stations, break down quickly in space. (know)
5. Recently, scientists _____ the effects of microgravity on living cells. (examine)
6. They _____ that the lack of gravity can cause muscle, heart, and bone problems. (discover)
7. Lately, researchers _____ techniques that could minimize the risks of space travel. (work on)
8. However, they still _____ everything there is to know about the effects of weightlessness on the body. (not learn)

B **Pair work** What has been happening in the field of medicine recently? Write sentences with the present perfect and the present perfect continuous for the words below. Then discuss your ideas with a partner.

doctors   hospitals patients insurance
experiments medicine research expenses

Some doctors have been allowing people to bring their pets with them to the hospital.

That's a great idea. Anything that helps patients feel more comfortable and relaxed will speed recovery. . . .

4 How important are they?

discussion **A** Group work Look at this list of inventions. Add two more items. Which ones are important to you? Which are not?

1. handheld computer game
2. VCR
3. pocket calculator
4. cellular phone
5. disposable camera
6. electronic dictionary
7. _____
8. _____

B Group work Imagine that you were putting things in a time capsule to be opened 100 years from now. Select five products or technological inventions that you think are representative of life today. Explain your choices.

5 Living without modern technology

discussion **A** Pair work Read about the Amish, a religious group in the United States. How do you think their practices affect their way of life?

The Amish

The Amish are a religious and cultural group who immigrated to the United States from Europe in the eighteenth and nineteenth centuries. They have preserved the way of life of their ancestors, following a strict set of rules for using such things as clothing, machinery, and electricity. Here are some examples of the way they live.

What the Amish traditionally don't do:

- have telephones installed in their homes
- own or drive cars
- have radios or televisions
- use electricity from public utilities in their homes (although they sometimes use windmills or gas)

What the Amish traditionally do:

- focus on family, farming, and worship
- use horse-drawn vehicles
- spend a lot of time with friends and relatives
- pay a lot of attention to their children
- stay informed by reading books and magazines

I guess that since they don't have telephones in their homes, they have to have more personal contact with other people.

B Group work Could you live the way the Amish do? Discuss how your life would be different if you did not have access to computers, television, or telephones.

reading **A** Pair work Discuss these questions. Then read the article, and check your answers.

1. What do you think the title of the article means?
2. What is a fish farm?
3. What is the meaning of *transgenics*?

Seafood that never sees the sea

Although 80% of the world's seafood comes from marine harvests, there is a major shift under way toward aquaculture now. Nearly 40% of salmon marketed today is raised in captivity, compared with 6% a decade ago. Forty percent of all clams, oysters, and mussels are produced in farm environments, along with 65% of freshwater fish. "The fact that world seafood supplies continue to increase at all is due almost entirely to the phenomenal growth in aquaculture," says Anne Platt McGinn, a research associate at the Worldwatch Institute.

Biotechnology is contributing to high-yield aquaculture through transgenics – the transfer of genes from one species to another. Researchers introduce desirable genetic traits into fish, creating hardier stocks. For example, some species of fish have a protein that allows them to live in Arctic waters. By transplanting this "anti-freeze" gene into other species, researchers have created more fish that can survive in extremely cold water. Biotechnologists are attempting to improve a wide range of genetic traits in fish used for aquaculture, developing fish that are larger and faster-growing, more efficient in converting feed into muscle, more tolerant of low oxygen levels in water, and better able to resist disease.

While aquaculture produces a reliable source of protein, the industry is rife with environmental problems, asserts McGinn. Perhaps the biggest concern is water pollution: Fish waste and uneaten food accumulate at farm sites and can float directly downstream into water supplies. McGinn charges that aquaculture also uses resources inefficiently. Fish farms need protein feed, and about 17% of ocean fish, an overharvested wild resource, becomes food for captive-bred fish. "An estimated five kilograms of oceanic fish reduced into fish meal are required to raise one kilogram of farmed ocean fish or shrimp, representing a large net protein loss," says McGinn.

Fish farming does not have to be an inefficient or polluting industry. McGinn predicts that many consumers will choose sustainably produced fish in the future, just as they prefer dolphin-free tuna today.

Source: *The Futurist*

B Group work Discuss these questions. Then share your answers with the class.

1. What are some of the advantages of biotechnology and other genetically engineered products?
2. What are some of the problems caused by using technology in the seafood industry?
3. How do you think these problems can be solved?

Lesson A *Entrepreneurs*

1 Success stories

starting point **A** Read the descriptions. Write the names of the companies in the blanks.

Perhaps you've never heard of _____, a company that sells naturally based oils, soaps, and other skin products, but it is estimated that in 1997–1998, the company sold a product every 0.4 seconds. Founded in 1976 by Anita Roddick, the company now has over 1,600 stores.

If you've ever tried to search for material on the Internet, you might have used _____, one of the most popular "search engines." Two developers, David Filo and Jerry Yang, started the company in 1994 as a way of keeping track of their personal interests on the Internet.

_____ didn't always manufacture cars. Sakichi Toyoda worked in the textile industry and first became known for the automatic loom he invented in 1924. He soon expanded his interests and in 1937 founded the company that now markets cars in 160 countries.

TOYOTA
Toyota Motor Corp.

THE BODY SHOP
The Body Shop International Plc

YAHOO!
Reproduced with permission of Yahoo! Inc. © 1999 by Yahoo! Inc. YAHOO! and the YAHOO! logo are trademarks of Yahoo! Inc.
Yahoo! Inc.

B **Pair work** Discuss these questions.

1. What might be some reasons for the success of these companies?
2. Can you think of other successful companies? What products or services do they offer?

2 Business disasters

listening **A**   Listen to two people discussing businesses they established that were unsuccessful. What are the main reasons each business failed?

Business	Reasons for failure

B **Pair work** Do you agree with these conclusions about the businesses in Exercise A? What other advice would you give people who want to open their own business?

	Yes	No
1. If they had opened the businesses in better locations, they might have succeeded.	☐	☐
2. They should have spent more money on advertising.	☐	☐
3. Had they started with lower prices, they would have attracted more customers.	☐	☐
4. Had they hired trained salespeople, they would have had higher sales.	☐	☐

3

grammar focus

Subject-verb inversion in conditional sentences

Use the past perfect of the verb in the *if* clause when it expresses something contrary to what actually happened. Use *would/could have* + past participle of the verb in the main clause.

If the company **had developed** good marketing strategies, it **would have made** larger profits.
If the restaurant **hadn't had** such high prices when it opened, it **could have attracted** more customers.

In more formal speech and writing, people sometimes invert the subject and the auxiliary *had* instead of using *if*.

Had the company **developed** good marketing strategies, it **would have made** larger profits.
Had the restaurant **not had** such high prices when it opened, it **could have attracted** more customers.

A Combine these pairs of sentences using conditional clauses. Write the combined sentences in two ways. Then compare with a partner.

1. I didn't go to business school. I didn't start my own business.

   If I had gone to business school, I would have started my own business.

   Had I gone to business school, I would have started my own business.

2. My friends and I didn't know enough about the potential of the Internet. We didn't start an on-line business.
3. Terry didn't develop a serious business plan. He missed a number of opportunities.
4. I ran up huge debts. I was forced to take out a bank loan.
5. Sun-hee rejected a scholarship at a language institute. She wasn't able to develop the skills to start a translation business.
6. Elizabeth and I refused financial help from our families. We weren't able to open a small cafe at the beach.

B Complete these sentences with your own information.

1. If I had taken a part-time job last year, . . .
2. If all the students in the class had started a small business at the beginning of the school year, . . .
3. Had I known more about the Internet, . . .
4. Had I followed my parents' advice, . . .
5. If I had invested some money in the stock market five years ago, . . .
6. If I had been able to predict the future, two years ago I . . .
7. Had I followed my intuition, . . .
8. If I'd started my own business, . . .

C **Group work** Discuss your answers to Exercise B. Ask and answer follow-up questions.

> If I had taken a part-time job last year, I could have afforded a vacation to Hawaii.

> Maybe, but wouldn't you have had a lot less free time?

Working at home

discussion **A** **Pair work** Look at these examples of people who work at home, and discuss the questions.

music teacher

"I love working at home. I set my own hours."

writer

"I need to work alone, so this is perfect for me."

lawyer

"Working at home means I don't have to spend money on a fancy office."

1. What other reasons might each person have for working at home?
2. What are some of the advantages and disadvantages of having a home-based business or profession?
3. Would you prefer running your own business or working for a good company? Why?

B **Group work** Join another pair. Suggest three businesses you could run from home. What problems might you encounter with each business, and how would you overcome each problem?

5

Entrepreneur beware

discussion Read these slogans for work-at-home advertisements. Match the slogans with their meanings, and then discuss the questions below.

SLOGANS	MEANING
1. *"Earn hundreds in your spare time!"* __b__	a. You are especially privileged to learn about this opportunity.
2. *"This huge, untapped market is waiting for you!"* ____	b. You can earn big money with little effort.
3. *"Only $29.95 will bring you thousands in earning power!"* ____	c. The market for your work already exists.
4. *"Our people have come from all walks of life and have succeeded with no special training!"* ____	d. A small investment will bring you a large income.
5. *"This valuable information has not been shared with the general public before!"* ____	e. Many others just like you have succeeded.

1. Have you ever seen advertisements like these?
2. Who do you think is attracted to these types of ads? Why?
3. Do you think there is any truth to what each ad is proposing?

writing

Business letters are written in a formal style. They don't include personal information that is irrelevant to the topic. Unlike personal letters, business letters tend to avoid contractions and idioms. Note that a business letter has five parts.

1. The **heading** includes your address and the date. It typically goes in the top left corner. If you use letterhead stationery, only the date is typed in, as in the example below.
2. The **inside address** is below the heading. It contains the addressee's name, title (if you know it), and address.
3. For the **greeting**, you should write "Dear" and "Mr." or "Ms." along with the person's family name. If you don't have a specific person to contact, write "Dear Sir or Madam." The greeting is usually followed by a colon (:).
4. The **body** of the letter follows. The first paragraph is used to state the reason for the letter. The paragraphs that follow should each focus on only one point. The letter generally concludes by thanking the reader in some way.
5. The **closing** includes a closing phrase, your signature, and your name and title.

A Read this business letter, and label the five parts listed in the box.

SUMMER HOLIDAY PROGRAMS
P.O.BOX 1234 NEW YORK. NY 10011 (212) 555-3900

December 15, 2000

Mr. Jonathan Hayes
1472 Park Avenue
Summit, NJ 07901

Dear Mr. Hayes:

Thank you for your request for information concerning our summer study-abroad programs. I am enclosing our latest brochure and an application form with this letter.

If you choose to apply, please make sure to indicate when you would like to begin the course and whether or not you would like to participate in our homestay program. You will notice that we offer both homestays and dormitory options for all of our programs.

As our courses are quite popular, they often fill up quickly. Please be sure to provide first- and second-choice starting dates for the program you choose. We will do our very best to provide you with the program that you want.

Thank you again for your interest in our summer study-abroad programs. If you have any questions, please feel free to contact me directly. I look forward to hearing from you.

Sincerely,

Donna Malnick

Donna Malnick
Program Director

B Imagine that you are interested in a study-abroad program. Write a business letter to the program director expressing your interest and requesting information. Make sure to include all five parts of a standard business letter.

C **Pair work** Take turns reading each other's letter. Label the five parts of your partner's letter. Suggest ways to make his or her letter clearer.

Lesson B · *The new worker*

1 What kind of worker are you?

starting point Read what these people have to say about the kinds of jobs they like. Who is most similar to you? Complete each quote with your own ideas.

Adam

"As long as I had the freedom to be creative, I wouldn't mind working in an office. This is especially important to me because ..."

Meg

"I'm not very particular about most jobs as long as I'm working with people. I'm the kind of person who ..."

Nick

"I can't stand sitting at a desk all day. I wouldn't apply for a job unless I could work outdoors. I enjoy ..."

2 The dream job

discussion **A** **Pair work** Look at this list of features of a good job. Add two more features to the list, and rank the items from 1 (most important) to 8 (least important). Share your opinions with the class.

The ideal job . . .

____ ◇ is close to my home or school.
____ ◇ has a flexible schedule, so I can complete my studies.
____ ◇ doesn't offer a high salary but isn't stressful at all.

____ ◇ has an excellent health plan.
____ ◇ doesn't require long hours.
____ ◇ gives you the freedom to be creative.
____ ◇ _____
____ ◇ _____

B **Group work** Join another pair and discuss your answers to Exercise A. Why are these features important?

To me, the most important feature of a good job is the freedom to be creative.

I agree. I think that's more important than money because . . .

3

Adverb clauses of condition

grammar focus

Conditional sentences do not necessarily use *if*. These expressions are also used:

as long as   on the condition (that)   provided (that)   suppose (that)   unless

Notice the tense agreement in the following conditional sentences:
As long as I make enough money, **I can** put up with a job I **don't like**.
As long as I made enough money, **I could** put up with a job I **didn't like**.

A Match the items to make logical sentences.

1. Unless I had some money to get started, _f_
2. As long as I don't have to work in the mornings, ___
3. On the condition that I don't have to stay away for more than two or three days, ___
4. Provided that I don't have to pay a really high interest rate, ___
5. As long as you have an original idea, ___
6. Suppose a close friend wanted to start a business with you, ___

a. I think I'll ask for a business loan.
b. I'm willing to travel on business.
c. I enjoy working at home.
d. how would you react?
e. you have a good chance of succeeding in business.
f. I would never open my own business.

B Complete these sentences with your own information. Then compare with a partner.

1. I wouldn't want to work as a stockbroker unless . . .

   I wouldn't want to work as a stockbroker unless I could make a lot of money.

2. Provided a company paid for my commute, I . . .
3. As long as I like what I do at work, I . . .
4. I wouldn't quit a job where I feel comfortable unless . . .
5. As long as my job pays well, I . . .
6. I would agree to work overtime on the condition that . . .

C **Group work** Discuss your answers to Exercise B. Ask and answer follow-up questions.

A: I wouldn't want to work as a stockbroker unless I could make a lot of money in just a few years and then retire.
B: Why do you think the stock market is so bad? I think it could be a good place to work.
C: Yes, but it's not for everyone. I personally would rather . . .

Essential qualities

vocabulary

A Choose three qualities that are important to working alone successfully and three that are important to working with others. Write them in the chart.

A successful worker . . . .

has initiative   **has charisma**   **has good communication skills**

is adaptable   **has specialized training**

is optimistic   **has leadership ability**

believes in honesty   **is innovative**

has influence   **has self-control**

is conscientious   **is trustworthy**

Working alone	Working with other people
A successful worker	A successful worker . . . .
has initiative	

B **Pair work** Discuss your answers to Exercise A. Why are the qualities you chose so important?

A: As long as you have initiative, you can make it in today's unpredictable work environment.
B: That's true. Things are changing so fast that . . .

Can you really learn that?

listening

A 🖱️ 💿 Listen to three people who participated in workshops on interpersonal skills in the work environment. List one thing each person learned.

	What they learned
Anne	
Thomas	
Paulina	

B **Pair work** Would you like to take part in such a workshop? Why or why not? Discuss your reasons.

reading **A** Pair work Do all your friends have similar temperaments, or are they different from each other in many ways? Make a list of three different kinds of people according to their values and temperament. Then read the article, and compare your ideas with the author's.

The Value of Difference

Every person is unique. We work with many people who are different from us. It is important to realize that differences are good and to appreciate that not all people are like us. On a team, the strengths of one worker can overcome the weaknesses of another. The balance created by such variety makes a team stronger.

There are three basic ways that people differ from one another: values, temperament, and individual diversity (gender, age, etc.).

One major difference among workers is personal values. Values are the importance that we give to ideas, things, or people. While our values may be quite different, organizational behavior expert Stephen Robbins suggests that people fall into one of three general categories:

Traditionalists. People in this category value hard work, doing things the way they've always been done, loyalty to the organization, and the authority of leaders.

Humanists. People in this category value quality of life, autonomy, loyalty to self, and leaders who are attentive to workers' needs.

Pragmatists. People in this category value success, achievement, loyalty to career, and leaders who reward people for hard work.

Another important way in which people differ is temperament. Your temperament is the distinctive way you think, feel, and react to the world. All of us have our own individual temperaments. However, experts have found that it is easier to understand the differences in temperament by classifying people into four categories:

Optimists. People with this temperament must be free and not tied down. They're impulsive, they enjoy the immediate, and they like working with things. The optimist is generous and cheerful and enjoys action for action's sake.

Realists. People with this temperament like to belong to groups. They have a strong sense of obligation and are committed to society's standards. The realist is serious, likes order, and finds traditions important.

Pragmatists. People with this temperament like to control things and want to be highly competitive. The pragmatist is self-critical, strives for excellence, focuses on the future, and is highly creative.

Idealists. People with this temperament want to know the meaning of things. They appreciate others and get along well with people of all temperaments. The idealist is romantic, writes fluently, and values integrity.

Source: *Job Savvy: How to Be a Success at Work* by LaVerne Ludden

B Group work Discuss these questions. Then share your answers with the class.

1. What kind of temperament do you have? Go through the descriptions in the article, and circle the parts in each style that apply to you. Do you know anyone who fits into any of the categories in the article?
2. Which category of people would you prefer to work with? Suggest ways to avoid possible conflicts with someone at work or in school who is very different from you.

1 Subject-verb agreement in sentences with quantifiers

Complete these sentences with the correct form of the verb in parentheses. Then add a statement of your own to each sentence.

1. A lot of people __*rehearse*__ what they say before giving a speech. (rehearse)
2. None of my friends _____ trouble expressing ideas in writing. (have)
3. The majority of people I know _____ interested in improving their speaking skills. (be)
4. In bilingual countries, the majority usually _____ its language. (impose)
5. At least half of the world's population _____ more than one language. (speak)

2 Overview of passives

Rewrite the active sentences in the passive and the passive sentences in the active.

1. I've been told by teachers that keeping a journal helps develop effective writing skills.

   Teachers have told me that keeping a journal helps develop effective writing skills.

2. My friends constantly encourage me to think more about how to use my language in business.
3. People often warn me not to think too much about grammar when I speak.
4. I've been told by people that it's important to develop my own speaking style in English.
5. My classmate told me to watch movies in English in order to learn slang.

3 Passive with modals

Pair work Complete these sentences in the passive using the verbs in parentheses and your own ideas. Then compare and discuss with a partner.

1. Languages _____ (could/learn) more quickly if . . .

   Languages could be learned more quickly if there were more language exchange programs.

2. A more extensive vocabulary _____ (might/acquire) more rapidly if . . .
3. Students _____ (should/tell) when . . .
4. We all _____ (could/make) to feel more confident if . . .
5. Finally, we _____ (should/encourage) to . . .

4 Indefinite and definite articles

A Complete these sentences with *the* if necessary. Put an X by sentences that do not need an article.

1. __*X*__ laptop computers have revolutionized business practices as well as daily life.
2. _____ computers of a generation ago seem like toys compared to _____ modern computers we use now.
3. It's difficult to use _____ computers unless you understand _____ technology behind them.
4. People invest lots of money in _____ high-speed computers they don't really need.
5. People spend too much time using and discussing _____ computers these days.

B Pair work Do you agree with the statements above? Why or why not?

5 Present perfect and present perfect continuous tenses

Fill in the blanks with the present perfect or the present perfect continuous of the verbs in parentheses. More than one answer may be possible.

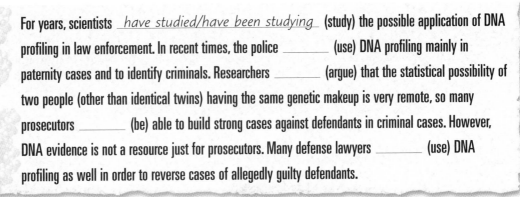

For years, scientists _have studied/have been studying_ (study) the possible application of DNA profiling in law enforcement. In recent times, the police _____ (use) DNA profiling mainly in paternity cases and to identify criminals. Researchers _____ (argue) that the statistical possibility of two people (other than identical twins) having the same genetic makeup is very remote, so many prosecutors _____ (be) able to build strong cases against defendants in criminal cases. However, DNA evidence is not a resource just for prosecutors. Many defense lawyers _____ (use) DNA profiling as well in order to reverse cases of allegedly guilty defendants.

6 Subject-verb inversion in conditional sentences

A Rewrite these clauses inverting the subject and the auxiliary *had.* Then complete the sentences with your own information.

1. If I had started a home-based business two years ago, . . .
2. If a partner had helped me start my own business, . . .
3. If I had accepted a job in a large company, . . .
4. If I had not decided to study English, . . .
5. If my parents had not advised me to continue with school, . . .

B **Pair work** Discuss your answers to Exercise A. Ask and answer follow-up questions.

> Had I started a home-based business two years ago, as some people advised me to do, I probably wouldn't be in school now because I would be too busy to think about completing my education.

> I agree. Sometimes you have to say no to immediate opportunities and think about long-term goals.

7 Adverb clauses of condition

A Rewrite the sentences using the adverb clauses of condition *as long as, on the condition (that), provided (that), suppose (that),* or *unless.* Compare your answers with a partner. More than one answer may be possible.

1. I would work on Saturdays only if they paid me very well.

   I wouldn't work on Saturdays unless they paid me very well.

2. If I could visit interesting places, I wouldn't mind a job that required a lot of travel.
3. If I had the opportunity to do creative work, I would feel happy working in an office.
4. If I didn't have to work with young children, I would enjoy teaching English in the future.
5. I would refuse to work for a low salary if my job didn't give me benefits such as a flexible schedule and the opportunity to learn new things.
6. I'm willing to work on weekends if my employer gives me more vacation time.

B **Pair work** Rewrite the sentences in Exercise A so that they are true for you. Ask each other follow-up questions.

Speaking tips

Group work What advice would you give the following people? Think of several suggestions for each situation. Then share your ideas with the class.

1. Gloria has been asked to give a short speech at a friend's wedding.
2. Hal finds he is too timid to join in the group's conversation after class.
3. Renata has been asked to give a formal talk about a topic she knows little about.
4. Wen Pin does poorly at job interviews because he becomes intimidated.
5. Joanne sits quietly at meetings because she's afraid someone will ask her to speak.

> *I would suggest that Gloria write out her speech in advance.*

9
Technological advances

Group work Which of these advances in technology have had the most positive or negative effect on our lives? Discuss in groups and give reasons for your answers.

jet engine

Internet technology

space exploration

genetically modified food

human organ transplants

atomic power

A: I think organ transplants are one of the most important advances in technology. They've certainly had a positive effect on the lives of many people.
B: Yes, but they've benefited fewer people than jet engines or the Internet.
C: That's true, but for people who are sick, medical advances like this are truly a miracle.

10 Is technology good or bad?

Group work Read these opinions about technology, which appeared in the publications below. What's your own point of view on the issues they raise? Discuss in groups.

Technology is here to stay, and you cannot turn the clock back. Whether technology improves our lives or ruins the planet depends on what we make of it. People who want to get rid of technology contribute nothing useful to meeting this challenge. We are not helplessly shaped by technology.

Source: *The World & I*

There are a few rules of thumb for buying new tools and technology: Is the new one cheaper than what it replaces? Is it small-scale? Does it work better? Does it use less energy? Can it be repaired and maintained by a person of ordinary intelligence? If not, don't buy it.

Source: *The Economist*

We must name the enemy, which is technology. We must tell the baffled, bewildered people that the problem is not one of political parties . . . or the lack of family values or the rise of poverty, not even the rise of corporate power and greed. While they are important, it is rather the technology itself that makes all the rest possible.

Source: *Minneapolis Star Tribune*

11 Personal qualities

A Which of these people is most similar to you, and which is least similar? Share your opinions with the class.

Roberta

"I've been told that I'm a charismatic person. The truth is that I'm a people person, and I'm not afraid to share my ideas with others."

Li-Cho

"I'm very optimistic. I try to look at the good side of things, and I'm always confident that even the worst situations will turn out to be fine."

Alberto

"I've lived in three different cities and have attended six different schools. Yet I've never had problems adapting to new situations."

B **Pair work** Which of these are your strongest qualities? Which do you feel are most necessary to realize your own personal and professional goals?

adaptability
charisma
conscientiousness
honesty

initiative
optimism
self-confidence
self-control

I think I'm very adaptable. Since I'd like to be an actor, and the work is unpredictable, I think it's an important quality.

Phrasal verbs

Some phrasal verbs are transitive, and others are intransitive. Transitive phrasal verbs take a direct object, and intransitive phrasal verbs take no object at all.

Transitive: When things are difficult, Tony can always **cheer** people **up** because he has such a good sense of humor.

Intransitive: I introduced my school friends to one of my best friends from home, but unfortunately they didn't **get along**.

Transitive phrasal verbs can be made passive, whereas intransitive phrasal verbs cannot.

Dan **was cheered up** after Tony talked to him.

Cleft sentences with what

What can introduce cleft sentences and basic noun clauses. A cleft sentence with *what* has the noun clause at the beginning of a sentence, but it is possible to use noun clauses either in subject or object position.

Cleft sentence: **What I look for in a painting** is an interesting color combination.

Noun clause (as object): I like **what I see in this painting**.

Superlative adjectives

Superlative adjectives generally occur with the definite article when they come before the noun.

Sandy is **the most interesting** person at work.

The most honest person I know is my brother Bill.

The article is optional when the noun does not follow the adjective.

Of all the teachers you admire, which one is **(the) best**?

The popularity of heroes is **(the) greatest** in times of crisis.

The article is not used at all when the noun is preceded by a possessive.

Venezuela's **most popular** rock star was on tour last week in Europe.

My **happiest** moment was when I met my favorite author in a bookstore.

Reporting clauses

When the reporting verb is in the present tense, the verb in the clause that follows can be in the simple present, present continuous, present perfect, simple past, or past continuous. The verb form depends on the time period that the verb refers to: (1) whether the time is simultaneous with the time of the main verb or before the time of the main verb and (2) whether the time of the dependent clause refers to a current situation or a general situation.

Alice *says* she **believes** in ghosts. (simple present: general situation, simultaneous with main verb)

Steve *thinks* Alice **is working** too hard. (present continuous: current situation)

Ralph *claims* a black cat **brought** him bad luck. (simple past: situation before the time of the main verb)

Ralph *claims* a black cat **has brought** him bad luck. (present perfect: situation in a recent unspecified past)

When the reporting verb is in the past tense, the verb in the clause that follows is typically in the simple past, past continuous, or past perfect. The verb form depends on the time period that the verb refers to: (1) whether the time is simultaneous with the time of the main verb or before the time of the main verb and (2) whether the time of the dependent clause refers to a situation in progress or a general situation.

Alice *said* she **believed** in ghosts. (simple past: general situation, simultaneous with main verb)

Steve *thought* Alice **was working** too hard. (past continuous: situation in progress)

Ralph *claimed* a black cat **had brought** him bad luck. (past perfect: situation before the time of the main verb)

Such that . . . and so . . . that

So that can also introduce a result clause.

Television has become extremely important in the dissemination of information **so that** much of what people know comes from TV.

Cause and effect with participles

When using a participial phrase, make certain that it refers to the subject in the main clause.

Correct: **Containing a number of unusual chord changes,** *jazz* is often difficult for many people to play. (subject: *jazz*)

Incorrect: **Containing a number of unusual chord changes,** *many people* often have difficulty playing jazz. (subject: *many people*)

In the second sentence, the participial phrase cannot logically refer to the subject, *many people.* Such a construction is considered an error.

Relative pronouns in defining relative clauses

When people speak, they use both *that* and *which* for things and *that* and *who* for people. In writing, however, people prefer *that* for things and *who* for people.

It is important to consult a specialist **who** has practiced this type of therapy for many years.

There are many clinics where you can find the therapy **that** you need.

In nondefining relative clauses, when you are talking or writing about things, always use *which*.

Theater enthusiasts love New York, **which** offers a wide variety of Broadway and off-Broadway plays.

My friend Isabel wanted a simpler life, so she quit her job at a marketing company, **which** had a very hectic work environment.

Verbs in the subjunctive

Suggest and *insist* take the subjunctive with one sense and the indicative with another.

Subjunctive: I insist **that we read** all the reports on a number of different models before we buy anything. (state a demand)

Subjunctive: The salesclerk suggested **that Pat buy** an extra filter for his camera lens, but Pat thought it would be too expensive. (make a suggestion)

Indicative: John insisted **that his computer was** a good buy, although everyone else told him he could have bought it for much less. (state a fact or opinion forcefully)

Indicative: Research suggests **that advertisers are** able to influence most people's purchasing decisions. (communicate an idea indirectly)

Noun clauses with whoever and whatever

Whoever and *whatever* can also be used to mean "no matter who" and "no matter what."

The new director will have increased responsibility, **whoever gets** the job.

Whatever you do, please don't let the cat out of the apartment.

Overview of passives

A short answer in the passive voice with a modal usually includes the modal, the auxiliary (if there is one), and the appropriate form of *be*.

A: Why wasn't John hired for the job?
B: I don't know, but he **should have been**. (He should have been hired.)

Present perfect and present perfect continuous

Note these instances when the present perfect, not the present perfect continuous, is used.

For a single action in a recent but unspecified past time: E-tech, one of the largest Internet companies, **has hired** a new president.

For the end result of a process, when the emphasis is on the result: As of this month, our company **has sold** over 10 million computers worldwide.

Subject-verb inversion in past conditional sentences

Past conditional sentences are also possible with *might*.

Had I studied business in college, I **might have gone** into international banking.

Had enough capital been invested, the business **might have succeeded**.

Unit 4   Superstitions and beliefs
Lesson B   Believe it or not
I've heard that one.   Exercise 5A, page 36

1. d   2. a   3. b   4. c

Unit 5   Reading and television
Lesson B   Television
Popular shows   Exercise 2A, page 42

1. f   2. b   3. e   4. g   5. c   6. a   7. d

Unit 6   Art and music
Lesson A   The enjoyment of art
Describing art   Exercise 4A, page 48

1. c   2. b   3. e   4. d   5. a

Lesson B   The importance of music
Musical styles   Exercise 2A, page 50

1. e   2. d   3. a   4. c   5. b

Unit 9   Animals
Lesson A   A wild bunch!
Animal quiz   Exercise 1A, page 74

1. whale   2. frog   3. dog   4. goose

Animal kingdom   Exercise 2A, page 74

1. b   2. d   3. a   4. c   5. e

Unit 11   Science and technology
Lesson A   Good science, bad science
Scientific processes   Exercise 5A, page 96

1. c   2. e   3. a   4. g   5. d   6. b   7. f

Acknowledgments

ILLUSTRATIONS

Carlos Castellanos   91
Roger Roth   27, 54, 64, 68, 73, 103
Steven Stankiewicz   98 *(top)*
George Thompson   3, 8 *(bottom)*, 30, 56, 66, 79
Daniel Vasconcellos   7, 8 *(top)*, 15, 34, 44, 71, 88, 93, 98 *(bottom)*

PHOTOGRAPHIC CREDITS

2 *(left to right)* © David Young Wolff/Tony Stone Images; © Arthur Tilley/FPG International; © Michael Krasowitz/FPG International

4 *(left to right)* © John Henley/The Stock Market; © Adamsmith/FPG International; © Bob Torrez/Tony Stone Images

6 *(left to right)* © Telegraph Colour Library/FPG International; © SuperStock; © Telegraph Colour Library/FPG International

10 *(all)* © Steven Ogilvy

12 *(top left)* © Nancy Ney/The Stock Market; *(top right)* © VCG/FPG International; *(bottom)* © Arvind Garg/Liaison Agency

15 © Richard Shock/Tony Stone Images

16 *(top, left to right)* © Abilio Lope/CORBIS; © Photofest; © George Rose/Liaison Agency; © Chuck Jackson/CORBIS; *(bottom, left to right)* © Photofest; © Photofest; © 20th Century Fox/Courtesy Kobal; © Photofest; © Photofest; © Photofest

18 *(left to right)* © CORBIS; © Michael S. Yamashita/CORBIS; © UPI/CORBIS-Bettmann

20 *(left to right)* © Frank Cezus/FPG International; © Frank Herholdt/Tony Stone Images; © Chris Jones/The Stock Market; © Gary Buss/FPG International

21 *(top)* © Photofest; *(bottom)* © Scott Wachter/CORBIS

22 © Paul Almasy/CORBIS

23 © Bob Peterson/FPG International

27 © David Stewart/Tony Stone Images

28 © Jose L. Pelaez/The Stock Market

29 *(left to right)* © David Young-Wolff/PhotoEdit; © Joe Polollio/Tony Stone Images; © Michael Newman/PhotoEdit

32 *(left to right)* © Tom & Dee Ann McCarthy/The Stock Market; © Steve Prezant/The Stock Market; © Rob Lewine/The Stock Market

37 © Bettmann/CORBIS

40 *(left)* © Rob Goldman/FPG International; *(right)* © Stewart Cohen/Tony Stone Images

41 From *The Incredible Journey* (jacket cover) by Sheila Burnford. Copyright © 1996. Used by permission of Dell Publishing, a division of Random House, Inc.; *(photo of book cover)* © George Kerrigan

42 *(left to right)* © Mark M. Lawrence/The Stock Market; © Ken Fisher/Tony Stone Images; © Globe Photos

46 *(left to right)* Vincent van Gogh, *The Stroll, Evening* © São Paolo Museum of Art, Brazil/Giraudon, Paris/SuperStock; Jackson Pollock, *Shimmering Substance* © SuperStock, © 2000 Pollock-Krasner Foundation/Artists Rights Society (ARS), New York; Fernando Botero, *Head*, 1983 © Fernando Botero, courtesy, Marlborough Gallery, New York; Mary Cassatt, *Susan on a Balcony Holding a Dog* © The Corcoran Gallery of Art/CORBIS

47 © Jonathan Nourok/PhotoEdit

48 *(left to right)* Andy Warhol, *Twenty Marilyns* © Private collection, Paris, France/Lauros-Giraudon, Paris/SuperStock, © 2000 Andy Warhol Foundation for the Visual Arts/ARS, New York; Salvador Dalí, *Untitled* © David Lees/CORBIS, © 2000 Artists Rights Society (ARS), New York; Pablo Picasso, *Weeping Woman* © Tate Gallery, London/SuperStock, © 2000 Estate of Pablo Picasso/Artists Rights Society (ARS), New York

49 © Tom McCarthy/PhotoEdit

51 © John Terence Turner/FPG International

52 *(left to right)* © PhotoEdit; © Chuck Savage/The Stock Market; © George Haling/Tony Stone Images

55 © Tony Freeman/PhotoEdit

58 *(top)* © Spencer Grant/PhotoEdit; *(bottom)* © Ed Lallo/Liaison Agency

60 © VCG/FPG International

62 *(left to right)* © Jon Feingersh/The Stock Market; © Jon Feingersh/The Stock Market; © Cameron/The Stock Market

63 *(top)* © Paul Steel/The Stock Market; *(bottom)* © Jon Feingersh/The Stock Market

64 *(left to right)* © John Olson/The Stock Market; © Roy Morsch/The Stock Market; © Michael Keller/The Stock Market

70 *(left to right)* © Cosmo Condina/Tony Stone Images; © Bonnie Kamin/PhotoEdit; © Ed Bock/The Stock Market

72 *(clockwise, from top right)* © The Purcell Team/CORBIS; © Jon Feingersh/The Stock Market; © Cindy Charles/PhotoEdit

74 *(left to right)* © Larry Grant/FPG International; © Gail Shumway/FPG International; © Jeri Gleiter/FPG International; © Planet Earth Pictures/FPG International

75 © VCG/FPG International

76 *(top)* © Stan Osolinski/FPG International; *(bottom, left to right)* © Keren Su/FPG International; © Tim Davis/Tony Stone Images; © Manoj Shah/Tony Stone Images

78 (left) © David Young-Wolff/PhotoEdit; *(right)* © Mark Scott/FPG International

80 *(left)* © Bill Losh/FPG International; *(middle top)* © Chris Salvo/FPG International; *(middle bottom)* © David Bartruff/FPG International; *(right)* © Richard H. Smith/FPG International

81 © Owen Franken/CORBIS

82 © Stephen Simpson/FPG International

83 © Wolfgang Kaehler/Liaison Agency

84 *(top, left to right)* © Cindy Charles/PhotoEdit; © Ron Chapple/FPG International; © John Henley/The Stock Market; *(bottom, all)* © George Kerrigan

85 *(left to right)* © Jim Tuten/FPG International; © Garry Adams/Index Stock; © Tim Flach/Tony Stone Images

86 © Rob Lewine/The Stock Market

87 © Chromosohm/The Stock Market

90 *(left to right)* © Stan Godlewski/Tony Stone Images; © Michael Newman/PhotoEdit; © Michael Newman/PhotoEdit

92 © Will Hart/PhotoEdit

94 *(left to right)* © Masahiro Sano/The Stock Market; © Antony Nagelmann/FPG International; © AP/Wide World Photos

99 © Frank Pedrick/Index Stock

100 © Layne Kennedy/CORBIS

101 © Kevin Fleming/CORBIS

104 *(left to right)* © Ronnie Kaufman/The Stock Market; © Michael Goldman/FPG International; © Jon Feingersh/The Stock Market

106 *(left to right)* © Howard Grey/Tony Stone Images; © Don Mason/The Stock Market; © Anthony Edgeworth/The Stock Market

107 © Mike Blank/Tony Stone Images

108 © Bruce Ayres/Tony Stone Images

112 *(clockwise, from top right)* © Lightscapes/The Stock Market; © James Marshall/CORBIS; © William Manning/The Stock Market; © Telegraph Colour Library/FPG International; © Telegraph Colour Library/FPG International; © Telegraph Colour Library/FPG International

113 *(left to right)* © Paul Figura/Tony Stone Images; © Michael Newman/PhotoEdit; © Gary Conner/PhotoEdit

TEXT CREDITS

The authors and publishers are grateful for permission to reprint the following items:

14 *Kidbits* by Jenny Tesar. Copyright © 1999 Blackbirch Press, Inc., page 281.

16 Adapted from "Judging Faces Comes Naturally" by Jules Crittenden, *Boston Herald*, September 7, 1997, page 10. Reprinted with permission of the *Boston Herald*.

17 Adapted from "Judging by Appearances" by Annie Murphy Paul, *Psychology Today*, November 1997, vol. 30, no. 6, page 20.

22 Adapted from *The Ponds of Kalambayi: An African Sojourn*. Copyright © 1990 by Mike Tidwell, published by Lyons and Burford.

25 Adapted from "A Lesson in Caring" by Teddy Gross, *Sesame Street Parents*, November 1994.

37 Reproduced from *Supernatural Guides: Mysterious Powers and Strange Forces* by permission of Usborne Publishing, 83-85 Saffron Hill, London EC1N 8RT. Copyright © 1979 Usborne Publishing Ltd.

38 *(left side of chart)* "Category Share of Consumer Purchases of Adult Books 1995–1998," American Book Association, www.ambook.org; *(right side of chart) Kidbits* by Jenny Tesar. Copyright © 1999 Blackbirch Press, Inc.

40 *(left quotation) Cassell Dictionary of Contemporary Quotations* by Robert Andrews. Copyright © 1996 Cassell Wellington House; *(bottom chart)* Adapted from "Who's on the Internet and Why," published in the August–September 1998 issue of *The Futurist* (page 11). Used with permission from the World Future Society, 7910 Woodmont Avenue, Suite 450, Bethesda, Maryland 20814. Telephone: 301-656-8274; FAX: 301-951-0394; www.wfs.org

53 *Note:* This information is a condensed version of a listing in Kenneth H. Phillips's "A Stronger Rationale for Music Education," from *Music Educators Journal*, September 1993. Copyright © 1993 by MENC. Used with permission.

65 Adapted from "More People Are Leaving the Rat Race for the Simple Life" by Julia Duin, *The Washington Times*, January 22, 1996, page 23. Copyright © 1996 News World Communications, Inc. Reprinted with permission from *The Washington Times*.

73 "Shopping Goes On Line" © 1998 by Consumers Union of U.S., Inc. Yonkers, NY 10703-1057, a nonprofit organization. Reprinted with permission from the November 1998 issue of *Consumer Reports* for educational purposes only. No commercial use or photocopying permitted. To subscribe, call 1-800-234-1645 or visit us at www.ConsumerReports.org

81 Adapted from "That Others May Live: Canine Search and Rescue," www.Petsource.com

89 Adapted from *The Cambridge Encyclopedia of Language* by David Crystal. Copyright © 1987 Cambridge University Press, page 118.

90 Adapted from *Schaum's Quick Guide to Great Presentation Skills* by Melody Templeton and Suzanne Sparks Fitzgerald. Copyright © 1999 by the McGraw-Hill Companies, Inc., page 16.

101 Originally published in the October 1998 issue of *The Futurist*. Used with permission from the World Future Society, 7910 Woodmont Avenue, Suite 450, Bethesda, Maryland 20814. Telephone: 301-656-8274; Fax: 301-951-0394; www.wfs.org

102 *(Toyota)* Used with permission of Toyota Motor Corporation; *(The Body Shop)* Used with permission of The Body Shop International Plc; *(Yahoo!)* Used with permission of Yahoo! Inc. © 1999 by Yahoo! Inc. YAHOO! and the YAHOO! logo are trademarks of Yahoo! Inc.

109 From the book titled *Job Savvy: How to Be a Success at Work*, by LaVerne L. Ludden, Ed.D., Copyright © 1998, JIST Works, Inc., Indianapolis, Indiana. Used with permission of the publisher. To order, contact JIST Works, Inc., at 1-800-648-5478.

113 *(clockwise from right)* Adapted from "Neo-Luddites Question Technology's Value," *Minneapolis Star Tribune*, April 14, 1996, page 01A; Adapted from "A Bad Press for Machines: Cranks and Proud of It," *The Economist*, January 20, 1996, vol. 338, page 86(2); Adapted from "Technological Luddites," *The World & I*, July 1, 1996, vol. 11, page 18, copyright © 1996 News World Communications, Inc.